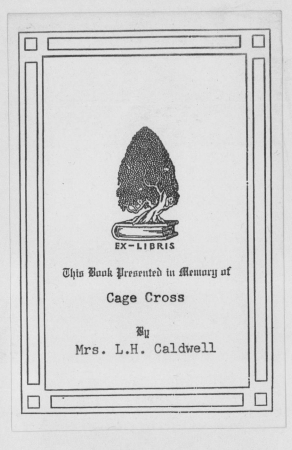

EX-LIBRIS

This Book Presented in Memory of

Cage Cross

By

Mrs. L.H. Caldwell

Forever Building

Forever Building

*The Life and Ministry of
Paul E. Martin*

WALTER N. VERNON

Foreword by
JOSEPH D. QUILLIAN, JR.

SOUTHERN METHODIST UNIVERSITY PRESS • DALLAS

© 1973 • Southern Methodist University Press • Dallas
Library of Congress Catalog Card Number: 73-88016
ISBN: 0-87074-142-X

*Of all that was done in the past, you eat the fruit, either rotten
 or ripe.*
*And the Church must be forever building, and always decaying,
 and always being restored.*
For every ill deed in the past we suffer the consequence:
For sloth, for avarice, gluttony, neglect of the Word of God,
For pride, for lechery, treachery, for every act of sin.
And of all that was done that was good, you have the inheritance.
*For good and ill deeds belong to a man alone, when he stands
 alone on the other side of death,*
*But here upon earth you have the reward of the good and ill that
 was done by those who have gone before you.*
*And all that is ill you may repair if you walk together in humble
 repentance, expiating the sins of your fathers;*
*And all that was good you must fight to keep with hearts as
 devoted as those of your fathers who fought to gain it.*
*The Church must be forever building, for it is forever decaying
 within and attacked from without;*
*For this is the law of life; and you must remember that while
 there is time of prosperity*
*The people will neglect the Temple, and in time of adversity
 they will decry it.*

> —T. S. ELIOT, Choruses from "The Rock":
> *Collected Poems, 1909-1962**

Strive to excel in building up the church.
> —1 Cor. 14:12

Knowledge puffs up, but love builds up.
> —1 Cor. 8:1b

*And now brethren I commend you unto God,
 and to the word of his grace, which
 is able to build you up . . .*
> —Acts 20:32

*According to the commission of God given
 to me, like a skilled master builder
 I laid a foundation . . .*
> —1 Cor. 3:10

Contents

Foreword

FOR SEVERAL YEARS I urged Bishop Paul Martin to write his autobiography. He did not refuse, but he did delay. After a while I realized he simply was reluctant to write about himself. I then pressed the point that he was a historic figure whether he liked the idea or not, and that he had an obligation to Perkins School of Theology at least to leave his informal reflections on his own ministry in the school's archives. He could not get around the fact that no other single person has been related to this seminary in as many ways as he—student, pastor, district superintendent, bishop, chairman of the Trustee Committee for Perkins, and faculty member. Further, he was the inspiration for the generous and insightful interest of Mr. and Mrs. J. J. Perkins in the seminary, he having served as the Perkins's district superintendent and pastor.

When Bishop Paul at last brought himself to prepare the autobiography, he did it superbly and charmingly save for too much modesty. The unpublished autobiography is entitled "The Humanness of the Ministry: Some Informal Reflections." A copy is in Bridwell Library at Perkins School of Theology.

Still lacking was a really adequate recounting of Bishop Martin's own achievements and honors, including comments about him by others. Consequently, I persuaded him to allow Dr. Walter Vernon to write a biography, using major sections of the autobiographical material. This volume is the result.

I join with the author in expressing sincere appreciation to the many persons across Texas, Arkansas, and Louisiana who have provided numerous incidents and accounts that have enriched this volume. Their names will be found in the various chapters of the book. We appreciate especially the fine cooperation of Dr. Hemphill Hosford, Mrs. Charles Prothro, Dr. Norman Spellman, and Dr. Decherd Turner, who read the manuscript in first draft and made helpful suggestions. As always, Mrs. John Warnick rendered generous service in providing resources from Bridwell Library. The author has requested a special word of appreciation for numerous courtesies rendered to him by the secretaries and many other staff persons at Perkins School of Theology as he worked on this project on the campus, and for the great interest of the SMU Press in publishing Bishop Martin's biography.

JOSEPH D. QUILLIAN, JR.

Perkins School of Theology
Southern Methodist University
August, 1973

Forever Building

CHAPTER ONE

O Little Town of Blossom

THE SOUTH CENTRAL JURISDICTIONAL CONFERENCE of The Methodist Church, meeting in Tulsa, Oklahoma, on June 14, 1944, had just elected Dr. Paul E. Martin a bishop of the Church. He was the second bishop to be elected that week by the conference, and both new bishops were from the same annual conference, North Texas. Dr. W. Angie Smith was the first elected.

Just as soon as the formalities of presenting the new bishop-elect to the conference were concluded, Judge Leslie L. Lyons, one of the delegates from another area of the jurisdiction, arose and read these lines to the members of the conference:

> The bishops grow, like weeds, you know,
> Deep in the heart of Texas.
> There's one right here, and one right there,
> Deep in the heart of Texas.
>
> There is no east, nor west nor north
> Deep in the heart of Texas.
> They just elect by word of mouth,
> Deep in the heart of Texas.

We cannot say we know them well
Deep in the heart of Texas,
But loud their praises we will swell
Tho' they are both from Texas.[1]

The charge that bishops "grow like weeds in Texas" was a gentle ribbing about electing two from the same state and conference—when there were eighteen conferences and eight states to choose from! Of course, it is true that Dr. Harry Denman, grand old man of Methodism, confidant of many bishops and other church leaders for forty years, claims that Texas bishops are a "special breed." Whether they are may be debatable, but in any event they were clearly in style in Tulsa in June, 1944.

Paul E. Martin gave forty-six years of service as a Methodist minister, twenty-four of these as a bishop, serving actively until retirement in 1968. What manner of man was he? Whence did he come? How did he serve? This small volume is the result of an effort to find some of the answers—even though partial and incomplete—to such questions.

Paul E. Martin's life and ministry as a Methodist preacher and bishop have covered three fourths of the twentieh century, during which time significant developments have occurred in church, state, and society. As he was reaching young manhood thoughtful leaders of the nation were questioning certain aspects of the American character and calling for a new assessment of values by individuals and the nation. The circumstances of his life were such that for many years he was to be involved in this ferment of reassessment of "the American way of life," in an effort to deepen the personal religious commitment of countless thousands, and in the task of helping to shape The Methodist Church more nearly into an instrument of God's will.

BIRTHPLACE

Paul Elliott Martin was born in Blossom, Lamar County, Texas on December 31, 1897. He was the son and only child of Dr. Charles E. Martin, a general practitioner of that community, and his wife, Willie Black Martin. Blossom was one of "the little towns of Texas," as such communities were labeled by Clyde Walton Hill.[2]

Blossom is ten miles east of Paris, the county seat, and at the edge of an area called Blossom Prairie in earlier years. It is almost on the line between the black, waxy land typical of most of North Texas and a strip of sandy land about twenty miles wide along the south side of

Red River, the boundary between Texas and Oklahoma at this point. It is on the Texas and Pacific Railroad between Texarkana and Fort Worth.

At the turn of the century Blossom was predominantly a farm area, the chief crops being cotton and corn. The only industrial operation was a cotton gin and cottonseed compress. The town had the usual quota of business enterprises—a bank, a couple of general stores, two drug stores, and an assortment of smaller shops. There was even a home-operated broom "factory" turning out a few dozen brooms a week in which the author worked outside school hours a few years later.

There were congregations of most of the evangelical Protestant churches, a good public school, and a Masonic Lodge. The citizenry was made up of a cross section of a sturdy stock, including certain professional persons and other well-educated ones. Paul's father and mother were in this latter group.

PARENTS

Paul's father, Charles Elliott Martin, was born in Maury County, Tennessee, on June 3, 1860. The family moved to Texas about 1880, crossing the Mississippi River by boat. The boat caught fire, but the Martin family escaped unharmed. The family included two brothers and two sisters of Charles who also settled in Blossom—Sam, John, Mattie, and Laura. Charles Elliott, having decided on medicine as a career, attended medical school in Louisville, Kentucky. Returning to Blossom, he gave his life to his profession, to his patients, and to his family. He rode a horse or drove a horse and buggy on his calls until his later years when he began to use a car.

Paul's mother, Willie Black, was born on February 26, 1869, in Blossom. She had a sister, Lillie, who became a deaconess in the Methodist church, and four brothers—A. P., who became a banker in Blossom; Travis, a doctor in Paris for many years; Ernest, a banker and businessman in nearby Clarksville; and Eugene, at one time a lawyer in Clarksville, for many years U.S. congressman from Northeast Texas, and for an extended period a distinguished federal judge on the U.S. Tax Court, now living in retirement in Washington, D.C. Willie taught in the Methodist Sunday school, and in the public school at Blossom before (and after) her marriage to Paul's father. She was Paul's teacher in his early years. Among her fourth grade pupils who remember her fondly is Sara Fryar (now Mrs. Max Wheeler of Paris), an aunt of Mrs. Paul E. Martin, formerly Mildred Fryar of Blossom.

In his "Reflections"[3] the son has written about his parents in these words:

My father received a diploma from the University of Louisville Medical School with the word "Distinguished" written on it and then returned to a small town to give unselfishly and gladly his life to all classes of people. Of him it could be said as was written of Edward Livingston Trudeau who did so much to treat and prevent tuberculosis—"To cure sometime, to relieve often, to comfort always."

From my father I gained the love for great literature. Our library contained the volumes of the finest authors. My father also helped me to see the possibilities of the use of time. Because the hours of the day were limited, he took these precious books and read them as he rode his horse to see his patients. What marvelous eyes he had to be able to read as the horse traveled slowly along!

My mother also taught me to appreciate cultural values, including the love for great music. Sometimes there were amusing aspects in the instruction. As a little boy I went with her to the World's Fair in St. Louis. A much publicized event was a concert on what was then the largest pipe organ in the world. It was before the day of baby sitters and a resourceful mother, in order to whet my anticipation, told me the artist would use his feet as well as his hands. How keen was my disappointment when he did not place his feet on the keyboard! A victrola in our home brought Red Seal records so we could hear the great musicians.

Across the years Paul Martin has felt a great debt to and loyalty to his small home town where he has maintained continuing contacts. His early years were the normal ones of a child who had the security of loving parents, a host of relatives and friends, warm and wholesome religious influences, and average cultural advantages. He participated in family events such as serving as ring bearer in the wedding of his uncle, Ernest Black, and Miss Robbie Lowrance when he was five years old. Mrs. Wheeler remembers him later as a popular, clean-cut boy with plenty of fun about him. In those years he spent his share of time reading the popular boys' books of the day written by Mr. G. A. Henty and Horatio Alger.

CHILDHOOD DAYS

His cousin, Louise Black, relates some things about the childhood they shared together:

In the fall, Grandpa [A. W.] Black always let us children pick some cotton in a patch near the house. I'm afraid we did more playing than picking. We often had "camp meetings" in which we would sing, shout, throw cotton bolls, and listen to the preacher. The preacher was always Paul. He would exhort us and we would shout replies and "Amens." After that we would go to Grandma's kitchen for refreshments of cookies, lemonade, and the like. I fear that it took the patience of Job for Grandpa to put up with such pickers as we were!

In my father's large "grass patch" (a cow pasture) we children sewed tow sacks together to make a tent of sorts. There we would create skits, jokes, and other entertainment features. Paul was generally the "barker" or announcer, as well as one of the performers. He had a fertile, inventive mind, and we had much fun with those shows.[4]

HIGH SCHOOL—PARIS

By the time Paul reached high school age, his parents decided to send him to Paris for his schooling. Blossom schools were good; there was once a small college there, attended by John Nance Garner (later vice-president of the U. S.) who boarded in the home of Paul's Grandmother Black. But the high school lacked accreditation for college entrance requirements. And there were several passenger trains each way daily which made it a simple matter for Paul to live at home and commute to Paris. Cecil Blackburn was a fellow passenger in the same class from Blossom, and he and Paul graduated together from Paris High School.

Young Paul made a good record while in Paris High School. In the *Owl*, Paris High School annual, for his graduation year of 1915 these words appeared under his picture: "He is of soul and body formed for deeds of high resolve." His friend Cecil Blackburn merited these words: "An honest man is the noblest work of God." Paul was a member of La Sociedad Español, president of the Sam Houston Literary Society, and he played the part of a retired businessman in the senior class play, *What Became of Parker?*

The impact of at least one teacher there was especially significant and is still remembered. He recounts it in his sermon, "Everybody Is Somebody":

Nothing quite equals the lifting power of someone's confidence in you. The greatest English teacher I have ever known was in [Paris] High School. She was Miss A. D. Johns. . . . Across the years I can still hear her chanting— "There was an ancient mariner. . . ." But etched in my memory is a time when she asked me to remain after my fellow classmates had left the room. I had presented an oration that day. She took my hand with a tenderness I had not realized she possessed. "Paul," she said, "You can make a great speaker."[5]

SOCIAL AND CULTURAL CONDITIONS

The Paris High School faculty had a number of outstanding teachers. Some of these had graduate degrees and Phi Beta Kappa status. Paris and Lamar County had many cultural and religious influences.

At the same time, that part of Texas was barely out of the era of outlaws and horse thieves. A. W. Neville in his *Red River Valley Then and Now*, reported that the U.S. District Court of Paris had a steady parade from 1890 to 1910 of "criminals of every degree—murderers, robbers, horse thieves, cattle and hog stealers, whiskey peddlers and what-nots."[6]

As late as 1920 two Negroes were lynched in Lamar County, and later there were two others in adjoining Fannin County.[7] However, at the same time there were friendly—even warm—relations between many whites and blacks.

ROMANCE

But in spite of these darker sides of life, youth dreamed their dreams, and fell in love. It was during high school years that Paul Martin and Mildred Fryar became close friends, and eventually sweethearts. They had grown up together in the community and the church. Hayrides for young people were among the standard social events of the day, and they began "pairing off" on some of them. As the friendship deepened, each found in the other those qualities that led them eventually to pledge their love to each other "till death us do part."

Mildred's father, John Madison Fryar, came to Blossom with his parents, Mr. and Mrs. Albert Sydney Fryar, a slave-owner in Ripley, Tiptah County, Mississippi. Mildred's father married Miss Ara Elisabeth Young, a beautiful and talented young woman. Through hard work and good management Mr. Fryar became a successful farmer and landowner in Lamar County. His farming interests were extended when he bought a large plantation-type acreage near Red River. The home remained in Blossom. Mildred's father died when she was twelve, and her mother died in 1919. Mildred was a good student, and was popular among her friends, according to one of her teachers in high school, Miss Faye Tankersley (now Mrs. C. C. Mason).

Paul Martin was acquainted with all the Fryar family, and after Paul and Mildred's marriage a close, warm relationship developed between Paul and her brothers and sisters. Paul became a real part of the family circle, and has shared many experiences with them. He speaks often of them with affection and appreciation.

CHURCH AND RELIGION IN BLOSSOM

The Methodist Church in Blossom was a significant factor in the Christian nurture of both Paul Martin and Mildred Fryar. Both families were active members, and we have noted that Paul's mother taught in the Sunday school. Pastors who served there while the Martin and Fryar families were in the church included R. C. Hicks, W. F. Bryan, C. W. Glanville, J. A. Wyatt, W. A. Thomas, W. H. Wright, R. B. Curry, C. W. Kavanaugh, Joseph D. Thomas, and W. N. Vernon. Brother Thomas has a special place in this story, as we shall see later.

Influential members in the community and church in those years included the families of W. C. Cassel, J. T. Upchurch, W. M. Gant, A. P. Black (Paul's uncle), S. R. Terry, Mrs. Emma Blackburn and her sons Herbert, Frank, Cecil, and Charles, Hugh Norris, Will Norwood, A. S. Fryar, Mark Womack, J. W. Abels, J. W. Humphrey, Max Wheeler, George Lowrance, Jeff Dickey, Robert Freese. Paul and Mildred were both active in Sunday school and Epworth League.

Blossom had a background of religious fervor. Just before and at the turn of the century the North Texas Area (and the North Texas Conference) was greatly troubled with divisions over the Holiness Movement. One or more great holiness revivals were held in Blossom. There was an active Nazarene Church in town in Paul's era. At the same time, the members of the Blossom Methodist Church had evidently come to terms with the movement, realizing that the controversy was not over holiness *as a way of life* so much as holiness as a *theory* or *doctrine*.

The doctrines preached and accepted among Methodists in those years of Paul's growing up were the standard, orthodox ones of evangelical Christianity. These included faith in God, based on acceptance of Jesus Christ as personal Savior and Lord (almost always through a public commitment in early adolescence), followed by baptism (if the person had not been baptized as an infant), and joining the church. Baptism was usually by sprinkling, except that occasionally adults would, on their request, be immersed.

Church services were usually referred to as preaching—and not worship—services, with the sermon as the central and most prominent feature. Lusty hymn-singing was a part of every service, plus moderately long prayers—by the minister at the Sunday morning service, but frequently by laymen at the less formal night service. The sacrament of the Lord's Supper was observed ("celebrated" is not an accurate term for that era) on a fairly regular basis, and the use of the Apostles Creed was standard practice for Sunday morning services.

Nurture was provided through increasingly effective Sunday schools for all ages and Epworth Leagues for older children, youth, and "young" adults. But the most common basis for church membership was the public commitment, possible at any service, but most frequent at revival meetings. The experience of commitment—often called "accepting Christ"—was conceived chiefly in adult terms, even for younger persons. "The call to preach" was also most frequently presented and urged at these revival meetings, at which visiting ministers often did the preaching. Dancing, card playing, and theater attendance were frowned upon by church members, though the prohibitions were gradually crumbling.

William A. Owens, in *This Stubborn Soil*, describes the situation he remembers around 1915 at Pin Hook, a few miles north of Blossom: "Mostly Methodists and Baptists, Pin Hookers were religious in their own way—fervent in summer, cool in winter—and industrious when they had to be. Those who could, made music. Those who could not, listened."[8]

John Harris, sexton of the Blossom Methodist Church, gave good advice one time to some of the members of the Nazarene Church in Blossom whose emphasis on faith carried them to what John felt was an extreme position. John was a well known and venerable character of limited capacities but sterling worth, who specialized in such services as rescuing objects that had been lost in wells and cisterns. One night at a Nazarene prayer meeting some were saying that the way to avoid smallpox was through prayer and faith. Finally, John stood up and said, "Brethren, I believe in prayer, and we must all have faith, but if you want to escape the smallpox, you had better be vaccinated."

Paul and Mildred were influenced by friends who lived in Blossom during their formative years. An attractive young teacher in the school had Mildred as one of her pupils. She was Bess Patience Crutchfield, who was then the fiancée of the Rev. A. Frank Smith, who preached his first sermon in the Blossom church while on vacation from Vanderbilt University. Upon his graduation Bess and Frank married and he took his first appointment at Detroit, just six miles east of Blossom. Their paths were to cross often in the years that followed, until the four lived in close contact in Houston, where Paul followed Bishop A. Frank Smith on the Houston Area.

As Paul was finishing high school, a new university was being created in North Texas—Southern Methodist University, in Dallas. Blossom Methodists, along with others in the area, had been called on to contribute to the new school, and every Methodist was proud of this new institution of the church. Not too many Blossom youths went away to college or university, but Paul's parents decided that they wanted him to enroll as a freshman at this new university in the fall of 1915. His horizons would soon broaden as he was launched into the beginning of a lifelong association with Southern Methodist University.

CHAPTER TWO

"O, We See the Varsity"

PAUL MARTIN entered heartily into school life as Southern Methodist University opened its doors. It was an exciting time to be in college—and to be at SMU.

NEW VENTURE IN EDUCATION

The university was a new venture for Texas Methodists. They had decided they must establish a first class university in a major Texas city, and they chose Dallas. Soon after the choice of a site was the choice of a president. Dr. Robert S. Hyer, president of Southwestern University, a recognized scientist and scholar and a widely influential Methodist layman, was selected. With the whole world (in a sense!) to choose from, Dr. Hyer began to build a faculty, and he attracted many who were excellent as teachers.

It was an exciting time at SMU also because Texas Methodists were (perhaps unconsciously) trying to learn whether a denominational university could maintain an openness to *all* truth—whether there could be genuine academic freedom in a church institution. Of course, they didn't get their final answer in those early years; that question is never finally answered in any institution of learning. Texas Methodists were also to face the question as to whether church members would continue to support a university after it became large, complex, expensive, and pluralistic.

It was an exciting time for the students, also, because they had a chance to help shape the traditions of the school. Perhaps most of what they did along this line was not done deliberately, yet their actions helped shape future patterns—and created a certain body of college folklore.

A New World for Paul Martin

For the first time, Paul Martin began to make close friends who were not from his own local area. They came from all over the state—and beyond. He began to learn what other Texans were like, and what the general characteristics of Texas and of Texans were. George Sessions Perry more recently has suggested (perhaps with tongue in cheek) that Texas is

not especially civilized, but . . . intoxicated with its own vigor, amazed by its own growth and wealth and bulging muscles. Its philosophy . . . the philosophy of action, gain and growth . . . The touch of exhibitionism [was] . . . a lively manifestation of our healthiness and youth . . . [along with] our staying power and our genuine if naive beliefs.[1]

Multiple Student Activities

Paul Martin began to learn what religion was like on a university campus, partly through the YMCA at SMU, which he joined as a freshman. By the fall of 1917 he was membership chairman. The *Campus* reported on September 7, 1917: "He will strive to enlist every male student in S.M.U. in the Y.M.C.A." In 1918-19 he was chairman of the Social Committee for the "Y." But he had many interests, and energy for numerous acivities on the campus. In the fall of 1917 he became captain of a newly organized "Cheer Club," later known as the "Rooters Club" (*Campus*, October 26, 1917). And about the same time he was named associate editor in chief of the *Rotunda*, the student annual.

Students presented a burlesque on the foibles of the faculty on November 28, 1917. J. Earl Moreland represented Dr. Ivan Lee Holt and Paul Martin played the part of a Captain Saer—evidently with great effectiveness. The *Campus* reported on November 30, 1917:

Captain Saer came to the stand, brushed the Bible and the song books off, and spoke about his war experiences. His talk was a long and extremely solemn one. At the conclusion of his speech he borrowed a cigarette from Dr. Holt, a match from Dr. [Hoyt S.] Dobbs, lit his cigarette, threw it away, and sat down among frenzied applause.

He became a member of Phi Alpha, which was then petitioning S.A.E. for recognition. He was on the 1918-19 debate team, being paired with John Cook. The two of them debated Hendrix College on May 19, 1919. Paul was described in the *Campus* as an excellent debater as they faced Hendrix, with the additional comment: "He has been prominent in student affairs ever since S.M.U. opened its doors." In spite of this buildup, Cook and Martin lost the debate. The *Campus* a week later explained: "They had a very difficult question to defend . . . and entered a contest that offered little hope of a victorious outcome." He was elected to membership in Tau Kappa Alpha, honorary fraternity of oratory and debate.

DRAMA AND MUSIC

Continuing his dramatic interests, Paul joined the Arden Club and had leading roles in its presentations. In the annual Shakespearean production Paul played the part of Baptista, a rich gentleman from Padua, in *Taming of the Shrew*. Among the other members of the cast were King Vivion, Ruth Hanson, Bruce Dickson, and George Thomas. On Senior Class Day in May, 1919, the seniors, of whom Paul was one, gave a very original program under the chairmanship of Gus Ford. In the program the class of 1916 was described as academic and aristocratic; 1917 was friendly but reserved; 1918 was rude, boisterous, and intolerant of the young class of 1919, which Ford represented as the most hopeful of them all. In a skit supposedly portraying the future, Paul Martin was shown as a vaudeville star! (*Campus*, May 17, 1919).

This interest in drama proved to be a lifelong one. Across his adult years his favorite recreation has been attending stage plays—in New York, London, Dallas—wherever there was opportunity. Only three days before his serious illness in October, 1972, he went to see *No, No, Nanette*.

M. Leo Rippy, a classmate at SMU, tells how Paul was selected as a member of the Glee Club.[2] Harold Hart Todd, the director, held try-outs and selected those he thought would make the best singers. Paul was not among them. Then Dr. Todd announced to those he had already chosen that one or two more could be added. Leo Rippy proposed adding

Paul Martin. Rippy recalls that Mr. Todd seemed hesitant at first about the idea, but some one spoke up, saying, "We have lots of good voices already. We just want *Paul* whether he is the best singer in the bunch or not. We just like to have him with us!" So he was added, and in turn added much to the group through his presence and personality.

Paul's membership in the Glee Club enabled him, along with the other members, to share in helping to create one of the traditions of the University—the use of "Varsity" as the University Hymn.

Paul was a loyal "Blossomite" while in SMU. A classmate recalls that frequently when Paul received his copy of the hometown paper, *Blossom Bee*, he would go through the corridors of old North and South Halls calling out, "Awake ye, good men. That great paper, The *Blossom Bee*, is here. Read it! Read it!"

PRANKS AND STUNTS

One morning when the students went to the third floor of Dallas Hall for chapel services, they discovered a calf tied to the leg of the piano. The administration was thrown into consternation, and diligent efforts were made to discover the culprits. No official report was ever made, however, of who the guilty party or parties might be. Bishop Martin still says to-day, "No, I did not participate in the tying of the calf to the piano . . . ," but then he adds with that timeless twinkle still lighting his eyes, "But I thoroughly enjoyed the strange sight!"

Dr. Hemphill Hosford, an SMU roommate of Paul's and close friend across the years, recalls another exciting episode in the college years:

In the school year 1917-1918, or it could have begun in the 1916-17 year, Paul began to show his enterprising nature for business. He secured the agency for cleaning and pressing men's suits which also included the laundering of shirts, linen collars and other wearing apparel. In time he found that students would buy "Stone's Cakes" from Stone's Bakery and milk around 9:30 or 10 o'clock in the evening. One could have said Paul would become one of the leading businessmen of Texas from these ventures. When South Hall burned in November, 1917, about ten o'clock in the morning, Paul and his roommate, Sterling Fly, at great risk of their personal safety, brought from the burning building some dozen suits of students which had been delivered that morning to Paul's room. Fifty or more students lost everything they had in this fire.[3]

Perhaps the most famous stunt in those college years has been called "The Great Mystery of 1918" by the *S.M.U. Ex-Student Magazine.* In the issue for January, 1925, there is a full account of the event. A scheme was concocted by Dick Dixon, Sterling Fisher, Hemphill Hosford, Sterling Fly, Douglas I. (Red) Maxwell, and Paul Martin.

The occasion was in the spring of 1918 during a boys' track meet being conducted at SMU for high-school students. The visitors were housed at the Adolphus Hotel, but took their meals in Rankin Hall on campus. The track meet had been somewhat tame, and Mr. Frank Reedy (then bursar of the university) suggested to some of the students that they arrange some kind of fun for the boys that might be remembered. He may have gotten more than he had asked for! The students mentioned above worked out a scheme that came off as follows:

While the high-school boys were gathering for their final meal, Paul Martin entered the lobby of Rankin Hall, hurried over to Dick Dixon, and began berating him loudly for something he had supposedly said about the *Rotunda*, which Paul was editing that year. An argument followed, grew heated and noisy. Friends tried to quiet them, but it grew worse. Finally "the lie was passed," as it is told, and Dixon pulled out a knife, whereupon Paul pulled out a pistol and fired directly and at close range at Dixon's heart. Dixon fell sprawling, his coat falling open and revealing a great red stain spreading across his shirt front. Friends rushed to Dixon's aid, got him in a car, and carried him away to the doctor as the high-school boys scattered wildly in all directions, breaking screens from windows, knocking a door off its hinges, and crawling across the piano getting out of there.

In consternation some of the other students chattered about what ought to be done. Some even spoke of lynching! Just then Paul reappeared, brandishing his pistol over his head, defying any one to come near him, and declaring that he was going to finish the affair.

Of course, it was all part of the prank. The bullet had no lead; the "blood" was only red ink. But it took a while for this to be made clear. It was reported that Mrs. O. W. Moerner, wife of a young professor and supervisor in Rankin Hall, fainted when she heard of the happening. Bishop E. D. Mouzon, dean of the School of Theology, called Dr. Paul B. Kern for the particulars, having heard that the *Dallas Dispatch* was preparing to get out an extra!

It took three ringings of the supper bell to begin to get the boys rounded up again for supper, and even then they would not eat until they had seen Dixon and Martin laughing together over the whole affair, well and friendly.

STUDY AND LEARNINGS

But alongside these times of fun—which were after all only extra-curricular—were many hours of serious study. As a freshman, Paul took courses in German, in algebra, trigonometry and analytics, in English composition, Western European history, and public speaking, as well as Old and New Testament history. In his other years he continued his public speaking training by taking advanced courses, including argumentation and debate and advanced debate. He took the famous course in Shakespeare taught by John H. McGinnis and continued his study of German with numerous courses: modern German literature, modern German fiction, Lessing, Schiller, and Goethe, and an advanced course in reading German. He also had courses in epochs of drama, and recent and contemporary fiction.

These courses in drama, fiction, and other literary forms were undoubtedly the basis for his later sermonic use of many selections from fiction, drama, and poetry.

He was also growing in his Christian faith and experiences. We have noted his activity in the YMCA, which continued through his college years. The North Texas Conference took note in 1919 of the impact on student life of the "Y." He attended chapel regularly along with the other students, and participated in worship at the university church. In his "Reflections" he writes about some of these influences and some of the professors he came to know and to respect deeply in his college and seminary years.

He also came to know many of the ministerial and graduate students, such as M. Leo Rippy, Harry S. DeVore, Earl Lightfoot, King Vivion, L. Bowman Craven, J. W. Crichlow, Ansil Lynn, Hugh Porter, E. E. (Red) White, J. Henry Bowdon, W. Harrison Baker, Robert W. Goodloe, Umphrey Lee, J. Earl Moreland, Hubert Sone, Sam Hilburn, J. Richard Spann, H. M. Hosford, Edwin Mouzon, Walter Towner, Joseph M. Connally, and Charles W. Ferguson.

STRIFE AND WAR IN THE WORLD

College students during these years were not unaware of the ills of the nation. The *Paris News* at about this time carried stories regarding numerous instances of racial strife, as did other papers; Negroes were usually referred to as "darkies" in the papers and never dignified as Mr. or Mrs.; a Negro was reported shot to death in a church in Osmulgee, Georgia, and the church then burned; a delegation of Negroes told the

Senate Foreign Relations Committee that serious trouble would erupt unless Negroes were given better treatment; John R. Shillady, secretary of the NAACP, was severely beaten in Austin, Texas, and put on the train under orders to leave the city; and the pastor of First Church, Paris, Dr. Bob Shuler, announced that he would preach a series of sermons on the evils of the modern dance!

Nor were they unaware of the war being fought to "save democracy." During 1917 and 1918 many men students volunteered and entered service to fight on the battlefields of Europe. The *Campus* for May 4, 1917, carried a headline: "Students Show Much Patriotism—No Slackers Here." On May 25 the paper carried a column headed "War Review and News from the Front." On December 14 it had headlines reading: "Many University Women Attending Red Cross Circle," "Students Urged to Purchase Thrift Stamps," and "Service Flag to Hang in Library."

In 1917 Paul started to run for editor of the *Rotunda* but withdrew in favor of two friends who were also candidates. One of these friends, J. Linus Glanville, was elected. But Glanville decided to enter the service and Paul was called on to edit the 1918 *Rotunda.* When it appeared on May 14 of that year, the *Campus* commented a week later: "It is by far the best *Rotunda* put out so far in the history of SMU. The key note of the entire publication is that of patriotism."

This same spring Paul ran for editor of the *Campus*, and won by a narrow vote. He still found time that year to be a cheerleader, to serve as vice-president of the Men's Self-Governing Council, and to sing second bass in the Glee Club.

In the summer of 1918, however, Paul decided to follow Linus Glanville and other friends by entering the service. He entered Officers Training School and was commissioned a second lieutenant. This made him miss the first semester of 1918-19, and consequently he was unable to serve as editor of the *Campus* as he had been elected to do. It is possible, however, that he may have been the only student ever elected to edit both the *Rotunda* and the *Campus*.

GRADUATION

The war ended in the fall of 1918, and Paul was back in SMU by January. By attending summer school he was able to finish in the 1919 class.

In March of 1919 a popularity election was held on the campus and Paul Martin was voted third place. He took part in two of the three

one-act plays presented by the Arden Club in April. When the *Rotunda*
appeared in 1919 it carried these lines:

> Paul Martin went away to war
>   To satisfy old Mars;
> Paul Martin came back wearing
>   The cutest golden bars.

But not all who went away to war "came back wearing the cutest
golden bars." Eleven SMU men had died while in uniform—three in action, one from an accident, and eight from flu and other illnesses. The
Rotunda was dedicated to "The College Army Man."

These college years were obviously stimulating and happy ones for
Paul. He had made many friends in the four years, he had "tried his
wings" in a variety of student activities; he had deepened his interest in and
appreciation of drama and dramatic episodes, he had cultivated his talent
for public speaking, and he had gained some maturity in the ranks of
the U.S. Army. As the college years closed he looked forward to a career
in law, a profession in which one of his uncles was finding a successful
career.

CHAPTER THREE

"Are There Any Candidates For the Ministry?"

UPON RECEIVING his Bachelor of Arts degree, Paul had planned to enter the University of Texas Law School. But his father was not well and Paul went back to Blossom to try to be of what help he could at home. His father had been serving as medical examiner for the selective service board in addition to his regular practice, and was also a member of the exemption board for Lamar County. The burden of so much work was telling on him.

FATHER'S ILLNESS AND DEATH

During the summer of 1919 his father's health did not improve. Paul was offered and accepted a position as principal in the high school. This was a fortunate decision, for he was able to be with his mother during the next fourteen months of his father's illness, and at his death on December 13, 1920.

His father's funeral service was held in the Blossom Methodist Church and conducted by the pastor, the Rev. Joseph D. Thomas, assisted by the Rev. G. A. Lehnhoff, pastor at Clarksville. Dr. Martin had died in Clarksville, where he had been stricken with paralysis two weeks

20

earlier. He had gone there to attend the funeral of his father-in-law, A. W. Black. The *Paris Morning News* for December 14 called him "a well known citizen of Blossom" and "a successful medical practitioner" there. Friends came to the service from Paris, Deport, and Clarksville, and a large number of blacks were also in attendance since he had served them, too, in their illness.

As School Superintendent

After a year as principal of the school, Paul was made superintendent. Assisting him as principal was his cousin, Miss Louise Black. Miss Black tells something about those years Paul spent in the Blossom school:

I remember that while we were teaching together the P.T.A. presented "The Old Deestrick Skule" to raise money. Men and women of the town were the pupils, Paul being among them. He was one of the funniest characters as he gave answers, played tricks on others, and so forth.

We also had minstrel shows, and there Paul was M. C. or Interlocutor. His exchanges with end men were always very funny. His speech was a rather slow drawl, and he could say amusing things with a perfectly serious face.

In school assemblies (all eleven grades were in the same building) he was a fine "barker" for our Halloween carnivals, class plays, and other entertainments. He could work the children up to a frenzy.

I remember that he entertained the senior class one year with a party at his home. To the surprise of the guests, he had arranged games of mumblety-peg, jacks, and other childhood favorites. The seniors became kids again and had a wonderful time.

In the April Fool paper that we sometimes published, he was a good sport in accepting whatever was said about him, no matter how far fetched the statements might be.

His wit and humor were often displayed in our faculty meetings. Mrs. Peecy Moore recently related an incident connected with her room—the sixth grade, I believe.

Though Paul was a fairly strict disciplinarian, he was always patient and fair. He tried to appeal to the best in students, and he set a good example for them to follow. He was popular with both students and teachers.[1]

While serving the Blossom School this educator made possible several rich experiences for the students—and the people—of this town not ordinarily available, at least in a town of this size. One year he arranged for Dr. Hoyt M. Dobbs, dean of the School of Theology at SMU, to come to preach the commencement sermon.

On another occasion he arranged for a brief appearance by former President William Howard Taft. This came about through a contact with a Chatauqua circuit that he had first made in the summer of 1917. That summer he had served as an advance man for the Chatauqua, which meant that he would precede the events by several weeks and start the advertising, ticket sales, and the like. He visited such towns as Royse City and Celeste. In the latter town he found his friend, Harrison Baker, serving as the Methodist pastor. It was from the Chatauqua agent he met in 1918 that he learned, while serving the Blossom school, that former President Taft was going to be on a train going through Blossom at 10 A.M. on a certain day. Superintendent Martin enthusiastically arranged to have his school pupils down at the train station at the appointed time, where they heard a brief message by Mr. Taft.

MILESTONE: MARRIAGE

These three years back in Blossom mark two tremendously significant milestones in the life of Paul E. Martin. His close friendship with Mildred Fryar had developed into a deeper affection, although during the SMU years their association had been chiefly through correspondence, since they were separated most of the time. A part of this time Mildred was in El Paso where the family had gone to try to find a climate to check her mother's illness, but to no avail. Following her mother's death, Mildred returned to Blossom. And on June 29, 1920, she and Paul were married by their pastor, the Rev. Joseph D. Thomas.

This marriage, as we have noted earlier, was no sudden affair. As early as 1916, J. Earl Moreland says, when the SMU Glee Club was to pass through Blossom on one of its tours, Paul went through the train ahead of time telling all his friends: "Boys, when we arrive in Blossom, there will be two persons at that station, the station master—and the girl I intend to marry!" Paul took immense pleasure and pride in introducing his friends to Mildred when the train pulled into the station.[2]

Bishop Martin reveals his deep and abiding love for Mildred after they had lived together for more than fifty years in lines found in his "Reflections," written in 1972. And he humorously writes that his father was the doctor who brought her into the world, and that as he held the little body and delivered the slap that brought forth the first cry, he looked up and said, "I want her for my son's wife."

Mildred Fryar Martin has conceived her role, as wife of Paul Martin (whether "Mr. Martin," "Dr. Martin," or "Bishop Martin"), to be that of a helpmate, as assistant in many ways, but one who preferred to stay in the background—lending care and support, love and encouragement, and sometimes advice. (They have a friendly laugh together as they each recall at times that Mildred once said to him, "Now Paul, you know I never fuss at you—except for your own good!") But "fuss" is not the right term to use to describe either her soft-spoken tones or her gentle manner.

Nonetheless, she has been an equal in the partnership. Although she has never been expected to serve as an assistant pastor, or assistant to the bishop, she has helped significantly by being the friendly, self-assured woman that she is. She has been one who could walk by his side with ease and with the kind of innate poise that breeds confidence in others. She has been equally at ease among the mighty of the world or among the lowly, with little children or with the elderly, the same friendly person with people who had much as with those who had little. Sincere appreciation was voiced when Hendrix College awarded an honorary degree (LL.D.) to her.

Although she deliberately shuns the limelight, she never shirks any responsibility. She has accompanied her husband to an unusual extent on his visits in homes, in hospitals, and overseas, and in entertaining guests as well as being entertained. The two of them have been noted throughout their entire career for the warmly personal relations they have developed in all their contacts and among all those with whom they are assigned as co-workers for God.

MILESTONE: MINISTRY

The second milestone referred to during these three years in Blossom was the momentous decision for a new vocation. We have noted Paul's early boyhood "preaching," his close association in the church, his many activities in church life, his good friends among the ministerial students. While in SMU several persons mentioned to him that the church needed persons of his caliber as ministers. Dr. Frank Seay, professor of Old Testament, was one of these. But the time for the complete commitment was not then.

The Blossom pastor, the Rev. Joseph D. Thomas, planned a revival for the community in 1922. He organized and sponsored prayer circles of four persons each for several months among the church members. The influence of these circles spread across the town. Then he invited the Rev. Frank Neal, pastor at Canyon, Texas, to come and preach for a series of revival services. During these services four young men of Blossom volunteered for full-time ministry: Paul E. Martin, Harry Talmadge Gant, G. Emmett Camster, and Herbert Norris, all but Norris being Methodists.[3] Paul tells about this decision in his "Reflections."

This decision for the ministry had been in the making for many years. In fact, all the experiences of his life up to that point had culminated in this new vocational choice. It was rooted partly in his father's example as a healer of persons, for in those days (as is still true in many instances) the family doctor not only healed the body, but also served as a counselor and as a confidant in moments of joyous as well as tragic and traumatic emotional experiences in the lives of his patients. It was rooted partly in the example of his mother as a teacher with deep concern for individuals. It was rooted partly in the examples of still others, perhaps the lay men and women of Blossom, fellow students at SMU, and especially, perhaps, some of his pastors, including the beloved "Brother Thomas" of whom he speaks with such deep appreciation. From Mildred came warm encouragement.

SEMINARY: TO GO OR NOT?

Coming from a family of professional persons, Paul's natural inclination was to seek professional training for his chosen field of life work. He was urged by the Rev. Clyde A. Long, at that time pastor at Roxton, and by Dean Paul B. Kern of the SMU School of Theology, to go to seminary. On the other hand, the Rev. S. A. Barnes offered him "a brick church" as a place to serve if he would accept a pastorate and begin his ministry immediately.

This decision for or against seminary was a crucial one for Paul Martin's ministry. It was not altogether the accepted course for young preachers to attend seminary, though the practice was gaining in favor. In 1916 the North Texas Conference had declared: "So long as educated mind and consecrated heart make a great man the church will continue in the business of education."[4] In 1917 it went on record as commending the professors in the School of Theology as "devout and scholarly men." Paul also had before him the example of his doctor father who had sought professional education for his life's work. He already knew and admired many of the professors in the School of Theology.

All of these factors together influenced him in returning to Dallas for seminary training. It is interesting to speculate on how history might have been different for him—and for the School of Theology—if he had chosen in 1922 not to enter seminary but to become pastor of the "brick church" offered him by S. A. Barnes.

JOINING THE CONFERENCE

Going to seminary also meant joining the North Texas Conference, for Paul and Mildred needed the income from a pastorate. Paul's father's death had removed an earlier source of income, and furthermore, the old saying was no more true then than it is now that "two can live as cheaply as one."

Consequently, he went to Sherman to meet the Admissions Committee of the North Texas Conference (held October 18-23, 1922) in Travis Street Methodist Church, and on October 19 he was admitted on trial. Bishop John M. Moore was the presiding bishop, and he addressed Paul and six other new members briefly "on matters requisite to success in their great work." Paul Martin was to become a close friend and great admirer of Bishop Moore, and worked closely with him later on important issues related to the School of Theology.

The North Texas Conference in which Paul E. Martin found membership was, of course, his home conference, and he gave little thought to joining any other. Bishop Moore described the Methodism of Texas and the Southwest in these terms:

The homogeneity of the people had much to do with the extraordinary growth and buoyancy of Methodism . . . the freshness of the frontier stirred their spirits and brought energy, courage, and enterprise into the church. Advance became the watchword and achievement the measure of reward. This is so to this day—Action gets the honor. . . . Methodism moves vigorously in this homogeneous region.

This homogeneity extends largely to theological and Biblical views. They are conservative but not reactionary; they are progressive but not fantastically liberal. To be sure there are some fundamentalists and some thin liberalists, some economic, political, and social reformists, some world orderists, some pacifists, some racialists, but not many persons are disturbed thereby. . . . Isms do appear but the sound faiths do not disappear. Blight comes to the church only where solid doctrine is blasted.[5]

Such was the area in which Paul Martin's ministry was to be carried on. His first pastorate, starting October 24, 1922, was at Cedar Hill in the southern part of Dallas County, but near enough to attend SMU. He speaks of his pastorate there in his "Reflections." One member there, H. M. Bradford, wrote warmly in 1965 about some of the deep meaning

to him of Paul's ministry at Cedar Hill.[6] At the close of two years on
trial in the conference, Paul was admitted into full connection and ordained deacon by Bishop John M. Moore. Appropriately, the conference
met in Paris and his ordination occurred in his home district.

Paul and Mildred Martin soon made many close friends among the
students in the School of Theology and among the pastors and their
wives in the nearby pastorates. Among these were Paul and Elizabeth
Stephenson, Wesley and Inda Hite, Walter and Ruth Towner, and, of
course, the two Blossom friends who had chosen the ministry when he
did—G. Emmet Camster and Talma Gant and their wives.

The "theology" wives had to learn how to manage on little. One way
they did it is related by Dr. Walter Towner of Nashville, Tennessee, who
was a fellow student with Paul Martin at that time: "My wife, Ruth,
and Mildred Martin used to go to the grocery store together. Sometimes
they would share the cost of an item, then divide it between them. They
would often buy one pound of bacon between them, each couple having
one-half pound of bacon then to last them through the week."[7] But love
was young, hopes were high, and courage was strong, and manage they
did throughout the years of seminary training.

The courses Paul took gave him a well-rounded concept of the Christian message and of the role of the church in the world. There were
courses in Old Testament, New Testament, comparative religions, the
church and modern social problems, the history of Methodism, the rural
church, the Reformation, religious education, church music, homiletics,
the doctrine of salvation, the curriculum of the church school, and ministerial leadership in the local church.

Paul's grades in his courses were good, practically all of them being
As and Bs. It may seem prophetic that his highest grade was in the course
on "Ministerial Leadership in the Local Church," for it is on this aspect
of the work of the ministry that he has placed so much emphasis throughout his career—whether as pastor himself, or as presiding elder (district
superintendent), or as bishop.

After serving the church at Cedar Hill for two years, he concentrated on being a student for the next school year. But in August, 1925,
he was assigned to Maple Avenue church in Dallas, somewhat nearer
the School of Theology. Here he also served for two years.

Having finished three years in the seminary, the Rev. Paul E. Martin
was now prepared to move ahead in his chosen life's work as a minister
of the Gospel of Jesus Christ. He possessed the confidence acquired from

having been nurtured in a loving home, surrounded by friends and relatives who accepted him; he had a good high school, college, and seminary education, including a good background in public presentations in speech and in drama and debate; he had four years as an apprentice preacher; and he was married to a devoted wife who was completely sympathetic with his goals and aspirations.

CHAPTER FOUR

"Where Are the Preachers Stationed This Year?"

THE FOUR YEARS as pastor in the Dallas District were helpful apprenticeships for the young minister. He had frequent contact with other student pastors, and he had trusted advisers in the seminary professors.

CEDAR HILL

When Paul Martin was assigned to Cedar Hill the church had a membership of 209, and this increased to 243 by the time he left. The salary increased from $787 to $1,340, and total funds raised grew from $1,436 to $3,357.[1] One stimulus to this growth was through a revival meeting in which two fellow theologs assisted—Paul W. Quillian and W. Kenneth Pope.

One day during the revival the ministerial team was visiting in a home for a meal and the man of the house said to Kenneth Pope: "Preacher, make a beginning." The young preacher at first thought he was supposed to start eating. Suddenly he realized that he was being asked to express thanks for the food—and he responded appropriately before it was too obvious that this was the first time he had heard the expression.[2]

28

When the Martins were at Cedar Hill bobbed hair for women was just starting to become popular—though not among all women, especially church women. They knew well and quoted Paul's statement, "If a woman have long hair, it is a glory to her. . . ." (I Corinthians 11:15a). But Mildred decided that shorter hair would be much easier for her to manage, busy as she was with the home, the church, and occasional courses at the seminary. So she went downtown to Sanger's and had it cut as a "bob." She and Paul both thought the women of the church would strongly disapprove—and say so. Great was their surprise when they found that the women had already accepted Mildred—and the length of her hair made little difference to them![3]

One year the church budget was incomplete, and there was difficulty in raising it. Finally the last fifty dollars was raised when Mrs. Prudie Carrell organized the high-school students of the church to pick cotton after school and on Saturdays and donate their proceeds to the church.[4]

Bishop Martin recalls one occasion at Cedar Hill of the sort that "try men's souls":

Well do we remember that afternoon when a stone from a nearby place was thrown by a blast and spiraled down the chimney of our house dislodging the soot that had accumulated in a fifty-year period. I was at school. Mildred was preparing the supper that night to be served to the stewards and their wives. I arrived thirty minutes after the disaster. The house was fogged up, my wife's face was black, with white rivulets made by the tears. But we entertained our guests. No wonder she made an outstanding preacher's wife!

At Cedar Hill a meaningful friendship was formed with a gifted young couple, Murrell and Juanita Bennett. Over the years, Murrell became a distinguished architect, particularly in the field of church architecture.

MAPLE AVENUE

In the fall of 1923 Paul decided to concentrate on school and to take no pastorate. He was appointed as a student at SMU. But the next August a classmate, F. G. Seyforth, finished seminary and returned to his home conference in Missouri. Paul was offered the pastorate at nearby Maple Avenue, left vacant by Mr. Seyforth. The church was in an unpretentious part of town with a membership of loyal, hard working people. It had been served since 1915 by seminary students, and the members welcomed the full-time service Paul and Mildred could soon give to the church. A new parsonage was built, and all phases of the ministry of the church were strengthened.[5]

In a little over a year the salary increased from $846 to $2,000, and total contributions grew from $2,032 to $6,836, most of the latter being money raised for the new parsonage.

The young pastor found these years at Cedar Hill and Maple Avenue a time when he made many deep friendships:

Although Maple Avenue was one of the smallest churches in the conference, it nevertheless gave me the opportunity for fellowship with some of Methodism's greatest preachers who occupied the leading churches of an important city. Dr. Hubert D. Knickerbocker, a unique and commanding figure, was my presiding elder. He taught me the meaning of stewardship. Carl C. Gregory, a gifted minister who built the magnificent First Church, was gracious and kind, and thrilled me by inviting me to preach from that great new pulpit. The scholarly Umphrey Lee was pastor of Highland Park and provided a friendship for which I will always be grateful. Dr. George M. Gibson, Dr. O. T. Cooper, Dr. C. M. Simpson, Dr. W. D. Bradfield, and Dr. Ed R. Barcus were sympathetic friends who inspired me. Preachers nearer my age who meant much to me were Paul C. Stephenson, Wesley V. Hite, W. Harrison Baker, Finis A. Crutchfield, Cicero B. Fielder, T. Lee Miller, Walter N. Vernon, Charles B. Garrett, Marshall T. Steel, and Walter Towner.

HENRIETTA

In the fall of 1927, Bishop Sam R. Hay appointed Paul Martin to the church at Henrietta, a little over a hundred miles northwest of Dallas. This was a radically different type of land and society from the cotton and corn area around Blossom—and Dallas. Henrietta is the seat of Clay County, so named for the sandy, red clay soil; the county's northern border is Red River. When first settled this area became ranch country, and still is, but in 1901 oil was discovered and this has been a big factor in the county's economy. Strong Methodist families such as the Waggoners and the Halsells were among the early-day ranchers.

The Methodist church building at Henrietta was a large, imposing structure—and it is still in use. In 1927 it was valued at $40,000, with a $13,000 parsonage, both debt free. There were over four hundred members, and among them county officials, teachers, doctors, lawyers, and other community leaders. It was a fine opportunity for a young, active pastor, where he was challenged to his best in sermon creation, in planning ways for the church to influence the community, and in organizing the church and its various agencies to carry on an effective program.

It was here that Paul Martin developed initially his techniques and habits of sermon preparation. With a study where he could work without interruption each morning, and with Mildred protecting his privacy, he progressed in sermon building. The congregation included persons whose intellect challenged him to do his best. He adopted the practice of writing out his sermons, but was able to present them without being tied to the manuscript or seeming to be reading.

The year before he went to Henrietta the church gained 12 new members, only two of them by profession of faith. In his first year, Mr. Martin found the names of many members on the church roll who either were hopelessly inactive or had moved away. When these names were removed from the roll, it meant a reduction of 125. He worked hard to offset this loss, and reported 28 additions by profession of faith and 20 by transfer of membership. The following year there were 20 received on profession and 50 by transfer.

Henrietta, being the county seat, had a great many weddings—some of couples who wanted to be spared publicity. Bishop Martin reports on one aspect of this situation:

The county clerk was the chairman of my official board and he directed many who had secured licenses to marry to come to me. The honoraria were substantial. Mildred again was thoughtful when she suggested a savings account to be the foundation of a fund to take us some day to the Holy Land. It was a substantial amount by the time we moved to our next pastorate. There were times when we were tempted to go into it, but we kept faith until we realized our dream.

On one occasion a committee including Dr. J. Richard Spann, pastor at Abilene, went to Henrietta to invite Mr. Martin to take a position teaching Bible at McMurry College. He declined, for he had already decided that the pastorate was his chosen field of service.[6]

IOWA PARK

After two years at Henrietta, Paul Martin was moved to the church at Iowa Park. This was a different type of community—virtually a suburb of Wichita Falls, with many well-educated persons and an excellent church program, especially in the church school. Again, the young pastor sought to widen the ranks of members, reporting in twelve months thirty-eight received by profession and forty-one by transfer. The church paid him $3,200 in salary on a $3,000 goal. Mr. Martin was active in numerous community affairs.[7] Friendships made here—as in all his pastorates—have continued across the years.

Iowa Park was a delightful appointment in many respects, as Bishop Martin makes clear from this comment:

The oil industry brought the citizens there and yet it was not a boom or border town. The leaders were college graduates. It was the only church I ever served where each person who occupied a place of leadership possessed a college degree. It was a delight and challenge to be with them. They anticipated opportunities for creative efforts.

Mr. and Mrs. John C. Murphree were brilliant leaders of the church school. They challenged the most capable persons in the church to accept places of leadership. As a result they had an excellent teaching staff. A training school was held one year with the largest number of credits awarded to a single church in Methodism. John Murphree served the church ably in General and Jurisdictional Conferences. His wife gained the highest honors in the PTA in state and nation.

Mr. and Mrs. Miles L. Hines were typical of the numerous fine young couples who helped carry on the good program in the Iowa Park Church. They were about the same age as the Martins, and the two couples were involved in working on many projects together.

Kavanaugh Church, Greenville

Paul Martin was reappointed to Iowa Park in the fall of 1930, but about two weeks later Dr. W. T. Renfro, pastor at Kavanaugh Church, Greenville, suddenly died. After careful consideration Bishop H. A. Boaz appointed Paul Martin to the vacancy, calling him "a most promising young pastor. . . . It was quite a promotion for this young man," he added, "but he made good. . . ."[8] Dr. W. T. Whiteside and Dr. C. A. Spragins, older friends of the young preacher, were instrumental in the choice of Paul Martin.

Again, Kavanaugh Church and Greenville brought Paul Martin into a different type of church and community from those he had served previously. Kavanaugh Church had 945 members, nearly twice as many as Iowa Park. It was in a sense a suburban church, though not far from the center of town. It had about the same size membership as Wesley Church, the oldest Methodist Church in Greenville. At that time Kavanaugh's membership had a large proportion of younger families. Its educational and musical programs were outstanding. Greenville was also the location of Wesley College, a Methodist junior college supported (after a fashion) by the North Texas Conference. A number of the students were associate members, and several members of the faculty were members of Kavanaugh.

Greenville was northeast of Dallas, located halfway between Dallas and Paris. It had about the same population as Paris (25,000), was the county seat, and depended chiefly for its income on farm products, mostly cotton and corn. A large sign over the highway on a major street greeted travelers with the words, "THE BLACKEST LAND AND THE WHITEST PEOPLE."

Members of the Kavanaugh Church were soon busily working with the new pastor, although a member of Wesley Church, Vinson Morris, overheard an older member at Kavanaugh say before he got to know Paul Martin, "It does look like the bishop might have sent us a more experienced man."[9] This member—and the whole congregation—soon learned that Paul Martin was more mature than his years might suggest.

A noteworthy feature in 1932 was the excellent attendance at the Sunday worship services. Mr. Martin also reported that he had held a series of revival services at Wesley College, held a revival at nearby Quinlan, delivered a number of high school commencement addresses, preached the consecration sermon at the annual Conference Youth Assembly at Kidd-Key College, Sherman, taught in the district training school and in the Texas Pastors' School, and delivered the platform address for the Oklahoma Conference Youth Assembly. The church contributed a scholarship to the SMU School of Theology, and paid most of the expenses of a young pastor to the Texas Pastor's School.[10]

In 1933-34 a new roof was put on the parsonage, and it was repainted; in 1934 the three Methodist churches in Greenville joined in a union revival downtown with Dr. Charles C. Selecman, president of Southern Methodist University, as the preacher; and Bishop John M. Moore was secured as the preacher for a special anniversary on February 11, 1934.[11]

One of the unique experiences the Martins had occurred at Greenville; Bishop Martin tells it like this:

In our congregation we had an elderly man who was dedicated but a bit eccentric. He lived in a small community nearby but held his membership with us because of two daughters. One day Mr. R. P. (Bob) Etter came to me and expressed his affection for me and said that he would like for me to conduct his funeral service. I told him I would be privileged to help in any way possible, but I hoped it would be a long time before the service.

Then he said, "But I want it next week." One afternoon the following week we went to his home with other friends and his family. Hymns were sung, selected Scriptures were read, a message on the future life was given, plus a tribute to his faith and faithfulness. Although it was all quite unusual, on reflection it appears to be an impressive illustration of a man's confidence in the beyond, and a recognition that he is a part of a fellowship that embraces two worlds.

Kavanaugh Church was well represented among the delegates to the annual conference; they were elected at that time by the district conference. In 1931 those elected from Kavanaugh Church were Tom M. Bethel, Marvin Love, and Mrs. Paul E. Martin. In the four years following Marvin Love was elected each time, and in addition Mr. and Mrs. Bethel, Mrs. Ira C. Kiker, and Mrs. Martin were all elected from the church in 1934. In 1935 all of these were elected again except for Mr. Bethel.

In 1934 Mr. Love represented the North Texas Conference as a lay delegate at the General Conference. He had the same role at the Uniting Conference in 1939, and at the 1940 Jurisdictional Conference.

In 1934 the Quarterly Conference at Kavanaugh granted its pastor a leave of absence to make a long-planned trip to Europe and the Holy Land. Mr. Martin arranged for the ministerial tasks to be handled by the Rev. Ira C. Kiker, presiding elder, the Rev. Paul C. Stephenson, conference secretary of education, and the Rev. Walter N. Vernon, pastor at Lakewood Church, Dallas. The church gave the Martins a new camera for the trip. On their return they reported on their experiences to several Kavanaugh groups and to other nearby churches.

In April, 1935, Paul Martin secured Bishop A. Frank Smith as preacher for a revival meeting at the church. Paul Martin was also in continuing demand in these years as speaker and preacher—at revival services at Denton and Sulphur Springs, at several high schools, Wesley College, East Texas State Teachers College in Commerce, North Texas Conference Youth Assembly, North Texas Conference Adult Assembly, and for several other occasions in the Paris and Wichita Falls Districts.

The strength of the educational program was noteworthy during Paul Martin's years at Kavanaugh. He supported each phase of it, reporting periodically that he had preached on Christian education, had observed College Day, and had participated in various educational enterprises. The Kavanaugh church school during his pastorate at one point had an average attendance of 405 with an enrollment of 565; church wide, attendance usually averages only about 50 percent of enrollment. In 1935

Mrs. Martin was serving as superintendent of the young people's division. The youth division had an annual banquet; the church had an annual vacation church school. In his report to the Quarterly Conference, October 1, 1935, Tom Bethel wrote, "We are deeply indebted to Bro. Martin for his interest and help in carrying on the work of the church school."

The five years at Kavanaugh were transforming ones for the young couple. They felt the lifting power of dedicated men and women who demonstrated the love and confidence of a great church.

PRESIDING ELDER, WICHITA FALLS DISTRICT

When Bishop A. Frank Smith assumed the episcopal direction of the North Texas Conference in 1934, he named new presiding elders on four of the eight districts. In 1935 he named new ones on two of the remaining ones. One of the latter appointments was Paul E. Martin to the Wichita Falls District. He had finished five good years in Greenville; membership had increased by two hundred persons, and the general finances of the church had become stabilized, in spite of the depression, after the salary had been reduced from $4,000 to $3,600. When the stewards offered to raise it back up, he demurred.[12]

These three years on the Wichita Falls District brought Dr. Martin, as he was now being called, into close contact with many types of churches. The types ranged all the way from the great downtown First Church in Wichita Falls to the five point Vashti Circuit that included, in addition to the Vashti Church, those at Newport, Postoak, Buffalo Springs, and Friendship. The district included the counties of Wichita, Clay, Archer, and Jack, and much time was required merely to travel over it.

As presiding elder Dr. Martin had responsibility for guiding the decisions as to how the smaller churches should be grouped into circuits— based on such factors as their proximity to each other, their financial strength, their spiritual needs, and the pastors available to serve them. He also had responsibility for seeking the best assignments for pastors, and ways of aiding them in their personal and professional lives. The Rev. Felix R. Kindel, a pastor who served in the district at that time, has testified to ways in which his presiding elder carried on his work:

Paul and Mildred Martin radiated their love for us ministers and our families. I know of several times he helped ministers with financial problems as well as other problems. The congregations of the district were always pleased to have the Paul Martins come. They enjoyed his preaching and felt encouraged by him.

I was teaching school at Newport to supplement my salary from the church. Wednesday before Thanksgiving in 1936 Dr. Martin came and called me out of the classroom to ask me to take the Blue Grove Circuit in addition to Vashti and Newport, that I was already serving. I resigned from the school that night to become effective the first of January. Dr. Martin promised to try to help me get appointed near Dallas so that I could finish my education. This promise he never forgot, and in October, 1937, I was appointed to Princeton and the next year to Renner, both fairly close to Dallas. Dr. Martin was instrumental in helping to work this out.[13]

Presiding elder Martin watched for opportunities to help younger ministers gain experience in the work not only of a pastor but of a presiding elder. More than once when illness or something else prevented his getting to a quarterly conference he would send a substitute. Several times he chose the Rev. Bill Morgan Smith, now secretary of the North Texas Conference, but then assistant pastor at Floral Heights Church. Mr. Smith testifies that these experiences were invaluable to him as background for his later years as a district superintendent.

The new district superintendent found a variety of types of preachers on the district—and came to appreciate the unique qualities that each of them possessed. He tells one story from the experience of the Rev. Earl Patton, whom he calls a "rare friend":

Earl became, wherever he served, a pastor to the whole community. He was in great demand for funerals. On one occasion he was officiating at a service for a rancher. The man had been quite a character; he drank, gambled, and used profane language. Earl was having some difficulty with his eulogy. Finally he concluded by saying, "Last night he got on his white horse and rode out into the sunset." The next morning the men around the store were talking. One said, "Did you hear about old man Jones' white horse?" When no one had an answer, he added, "He came home with his mane and tail singed!"

When Dr. Martin became presiding elder the district had 10,684 members, with 7,774 on the Sunday school rolls. By the time he left the district, membership had increased to 11,111, and Sunday school enrollment to 8,059. Similarly, financial support by the churches had increased from $113,882 in 1935 to $299,023 in 1938, though this was not a normal figure, since it involved extra large payments on church buildings, especially by First Church, Wichita Falls. However, for the next five years the average amount raised in the district was almost $180,000, so this gain under Dr. Martin's leadership was a real raising of sights on the part of the people in the district.

In addition to the benefits that came to the district from Dr. Martin's tenure, several advantages accrued to him. He came to know Bishop A. Frank Smith in an administrative relationship: what the bishop expects of the presiding elder, and how the bishop can help (or hinder!) the presiding elder and the local church. His concerns were now shifting from those of only one local church or one district to the concerns of the whole conference and beyond. He was becoming a builder in the deeper sense of one who creates or establishes. He had dedicated himself to building the Christian faith into the lives of persons, and a Christian spirit into the activities of churches and churchmen.

Perhaps most helpful for his future responsibilities was his schooling in the making of appointments. He came to see from actual operation of the itinerant system that appointment-making is based on an appropriate balance between the needs and wishes of the local churches and the needs and wishes of the pastors. These cannot, he learned, always be fitted perfectly together—yet the bishop and the cabinet of presiding elders (now called district superintendents) must faithfully seek the most nearly perfect placements possible. He learned also the need to consider carefully the sequence of pastors at churches—not every pastor can successfully follow every other pastor. These experiences were to stand him in good stead in his twenty-four years of appointment-making as bishop.

CHAPTER FIVE

"There Is a Man of God in This City"

DR. IVAN LEE HOLT, Chaplain at SMU when Paul Martin was an undergraduate, and pastor for many years at prestigious St. John's Church in St. Louis, was elected bishop in May, 1938. He was assigned to the North Texas Conference, and among his first responsibilities was the filling of two of the "leading" pulpits—First Church, Dallas, and First Church, Wichita Falls.

The Dallas vacancy was created by the election of Dr. William C. Martin as bishop (at the same time as Bishop Holt), and the Wichita Falls change grew out of the somewhat normal Methodist shift of pastors—Dr. C. M. Raby had been there six years. The Dallas pulpit was filled by the appointment of Dr. W. Angie Smith, native Texan and brother of Bishop A. Frank Smith of Houston. Dr. Paul E. Martin was assigned to the Wichita Falls church. The careers of Martin and Smith have numerous other parallels, as we shall see.

Dr. Martin was no stranger to the Wichita Falls congregation, of course, by virtue of his service as pastor in the district at Henrietta (1927-29) and at Iowa Park (1929-30), and as presiding elder for three years (1935-38). He was active in district affairs while serving as pastor of the two churches, and as presiding elder had preached some dozen times in the Wichita Falls church. He had also been closely associated with some of the lay persons from the church in his years on the SMU Board of Trustees, and when he supervised all Methodist affairs in the district while presiding elder. These persons had made known their desire that Dr. Martin be assigned as their pastor.

A RANCH AND OIL AREA

Wichita Falls is the second largest city in the North Texas Conference. It is a much younger city than Dallas, however, having been founded in 1879 by Judge J. H. Barwise from Dallas. Although Wichita County had been authorized in 1858, it was not organized until 1882. Large ranches were the pattern across the county; the area was known as a part of the "cow country." The great cattle drives went through this part of the country. Eventually a limited amount of agriculture was established.

Early in 1900 oil was found around Wichita Falls, but it was not until 1917-18 that the real "boom" arrived. For a time the city became a hectic and wild center for the frenzied activities of oil speculators, sometimes presenting a regular carnival atmosphere.[1] Gradually the boom period settled down into a more stable situation, and the population grew from 43,000 in 1930 to around 100,000 in 1972. This population expansion has been based on a fairly diversified economy.

There was Methodist preaching in Wichita Falls at least by 1880, and a church was organized the following year by the Rev. F. O. Miller.[2] It developed year by year, and by 1938 First Church, Wichita, had become a strong church, supported by a loyal and capable membership.

BUILDING ON THE ONGOING PROGRAM

The Martins were warmly welcomed by the members of the church and the parsonage was refurbished for them. The new pastor found a good program under way, a well organized Board of Stewards under the chairmanship of J. S. Bridwell, and a total church budget of $25,000. The pastor's salary was $5,000. The Sunday school, under the superintendency of J. W. Thorne, had a membership of over 1,300. The church had an outstanding record in its offerings to the Methodist Home at Waco, thanks to special interest on the part of such persons as J. J. Perkins, J. S. Bridwell, and Ralph DeShong. At Christmas, 1938, the offering amounted to $2,925.[3]

Dr. Martin proposed, and the Board approved, a Visitation Council with a general chairman, four zone chairmen, and five subdivisions in each zone. Its function was to provide visitation in each home several times a year for fellowship, evangelism, and other purposes.

When Dr. Martin arrived the new sanctuary had been completed and the small remaining debt was soon cleared off. On April 23, 1939, the building was officially dedicated. The pastor's concept of the purpose of the church—and in a sense, the role of a pastor—was spelled out in connection with the dedication:

It seeks to provide comfort for the sorrowing, relief for the distressed, deliverance for the sinful, hope for the bewildered, consolation for the dying, and challenge for the strong. It affords an opportunity for worship, for instruction, for fellowship, and for the expression of Christian service.

As plans were being made in the Board of Stewards meeting for the dedication of the building, Mr. Bridwell called on the stewards to rededicate themselves to their own Christian commitment. A homecoming celebration was held on April 22, just preceding the dedication services. Dr. W. Angie Smith of Dallas and Bishop Angie Frank Smith of Houston were the preachers at the services.

In connection with the dedication, Dr. Martin and the church received a communication from Vice-President John Nance Garner, which the vice-president sent partly because of his friendship with Dr. Martin's parents and grandparents. The message was one of national political significance, for it was his first message released after assuming his new office and constituted a dramatic break with President Roosevelt on economic issues. "In a subtle fashion," writes Dr. Martin, "he referred to the paying of debts. It appeared the next morning on the front pages of the nation's newspapers. It was an interesting way also of bringing the son of old friends into prominence."

For many years the chairman of the Budget Committee, D. Houston Bolin, gave outstanding guidance in planning and raising the church's funds. In the fall of 1939, for example, he proposed that (1) each member make an ongoing pledge rather than an annual one (subject to cancellation if necessary), (2) that each steward be responsible for collection from a specified list of members, and (3) that pledges be taken each October for the next calendar year. By the time Dr. Martin left in 1944 the budget had increased from $25,000 to over $50,000.

In the fall of 1939 the pastor's salary was increased to $6,000. It may be that some of the stewards had learned that their pastor was being sought for other pastorates, and wanted to be sure he stayed in Wichita Falls. Dr. Martin was asked by Bishop Charles C. Selecman of Oklahoma City if he would consider being named as pastor of Boston Avenue Church in Tulsa. His reply showed the strong ties between pastor and people in Wichita Falls:

I feel . . . I should remain here. We have been accorded a wholehearted loyalty and devotion on the part of the officials and members of this great Church that would inspire and challenge any preacher. I feel I would not be true to them if I left at this time. . . . We have much to do here, and the task is not an easy one, but it holds an attraction that cannot be resisted.[4]

Along with the increase in salary was another action by the Board of Stewards, phrased in the inimitable language of the secretary, Oral Jones, whose minutes are a joy to read:

Upon motion by most everybody in the house and duly seconded, the preacher was ordered to outfit himself with new toggery from head to foot, including new suit, hat, shoes, shirts, ties, collars, underwear and a brand new overcoat—all these expressions of affection, esteem, and love, were accepted with apparent little reluctance!

This action was a tangible expression of a resolution adopted about the same time, asking for the return of Dr. Martin and declaring that "at no other time in our history has this congregation been more happily associated with its pastor."

A PROGRAM OF WIDE SCOPE

The report of the pastor to the Quarterly Conference in the fall of 1940 shows something of the scope of the church's program:

Our commodious plant continues to be used for many purposes outside of our Church program. During this Quarter the Organ Guild concerts were again held here; the State Federation of Women's Clubs held its public meeting in our auditorium, as well as an organ concert; the Crippled Children's Clinic made use of our facilities; a number of District meetings, including the Watch Night Service, were given here; the Optimist Dinner for needy boys was provided in our dining room; the University of Scouting offered its course here; and the mid-year class of the High School had our beautiful auditorium as the setting for its Baccalaureate Service. Day and night our great plant is being used, as we believe, for the purpose for which it was intended by its builders.

During this period our Chorus Choir, under the direction of Mrs. Pearl Calhoun Davis, with Mrs. J. W. Akin, Jr., at the organ, has not only furnished the musical backgrounds for our services of worship but has sponsored a number of other lovely programs. . . . The A Cappella Choir of the North Texas State Teachers College at Denton again inspired us with superb music. A recital that was much appreciated by music lovers was given by Mrs. J. W. Akin, Jr. and Mrs. W. C. Hamilton. The Christmas program, "Why the Chimes Rang," was even more noteworthy, if possible, than last year.

The response of the Church to the use of excellent literature is indicated by the books that are being added to the Church School library. . . . We have sent in 117 subscriptions to the *Southwestern Christian Advocate*, which, according to its business manager, is "the largest number received from any church so far. Seventy mission books have been sold. . . .

Through the efforts of Mr. J. J. Perkins, the greatest friend 400 children in the Methodist Home have, and the generosity of the members of our Church, we are giving the largest offering ever given to the Home, $4,402.12.

A report of this sort is not complete without indicating future events that are worthy of announcement. During next week the great Methodist Advance meetings are to be held in our territory. One is in Dallas on Tuesday the other in Fort Worth on Thursday. Those who attend either meeting will be greatly inspired. A great Youth Crusade Rally is to be held at Floral Heights Church February 21. In our own Church, the District School for Christian Workers is to be held the week beginning February 25. Other meetings that will be announced later are the General and Jurisdictional Conferences, the Summer Assemblies and our own Vacation Church School. Easter comes this year on March 24, and in preparation for it we plan a class in Pastoral Instruction of Children, an effort in personal evangelism and a challenge to loyalty on the part of our own people.

Some physical improvements have been made this Quarter. . . . Consideration is being given to the improvement of our foyer, to our heating and air conditioning problem, and to the Primary Department in our Church School. We need an adequate social hall as well and appropriate pictures for class rooms and departments.

We hope to be able to announce the addition of a new member to our staff within the next few days. We are all convinced of our need in this respect.

During this quarter, in addition to his regular duties, the pastor attended the Stewardship Council and Conference as the ministerial representative of The Methodist Church; with the three other local trustees, J. S. Bridwell, W. B. Hamilton and J. J. Perkins, he participated in the inauguration of President Umphrey Lee at S.M.U.; he spoke at meetings or banquets at Gainesville, Henrietta, Iowa Park, West Side Baptist Church, Sam Houston School, Wilson Memorial Church, Crockett School P.T.A., Optimist Dinner for needy Boys, Hi Y Group, Boy Scout Parent Appreciation Dinner, Dedication of Gideon Bibles, Baccalaureate Service, and Watch Night Service for young people at Floral Heights.

This report is already too long, but I must not conclude it without paying tribute to my associate, Rev. Earl R. Hoggard, and our most excellent staff. The possibilities for good offered to this great church are unlimited. May we be worthy of our opportunities is our prayer.

Dr. Martin's ministry was a popular one, but the gospel he preached was not an easy-going matter. Shortly before Christmas, 1940, the Board minutes reveal that "our beloved Pastor delivered a blistering appeal to the members of the Quarterly Conference and to all the members of the Church to wake up from our apparent lethargy as to individual responsibility, and to come alive on the matter of the sacred responsibility of church membership."

This exhortation must have been taken seriously, for a few months later it was reported that the church had received more members on profession of faith than any other church in the North Texas Conference. "Dr. Martin ended his report to the Board by reminding us of the people who are entering the Church each week and of those who have been saved at its altars."

The concern and assistance of the church went far beyond its own membership. World Service and annual conference causes received $3,000 in 1938-39 and $5,000 in 1943-44. Special offerings were given to such causes as the Waco Methodist Home, Week of Dedication, superannuate home, Golden Cross, Camp Fire Girls, A&M Church fund, Gideon Bibles, janitor vacation fund, the local Gilbert Memorial Colored (now Christian) Methodist Episcopal Church, Pastor Anderson Chapel of the African Methodist Episcopal Church, and Mount Calvary Methodist Church.

The camaraderie within the Board of Stewards was significant. One notation in the minutes for May 5, 1941, read: "Mr. Perkins made the announcement that all who attend the next dinner and Stewards meeting in June would receive a complimentary bucket of Uvalde honey, from him personally, and to this announcement pandemonium reigned supreme."

A MINISTRY TO THOSE IN SERVICE

By the fall of 1941 the church was feeling the effect of the influx of servicemen at Sheppard Field. Several hundred of them were coming to the church services, and a special Soldiers' Lounge was provided. Many members invited soldiers after services into their homes for meals and visits. Mrs. J. W. Akin, Jr., the capable church organist, provided an organ recital for the servicemen and their families once a month. On several occasions chaplains from the base were guests at the meeting of the Board of Stewards. One soldier later wrote to the pastor in these words: "Spending my Sundays in your church made me see for the first time just what the church really means and how much it can help to keep people happy."

Bishop Martin recalls the values of this ministry to the servicemen:

Life was richer because we knew these soldiers. We call to remembrance many individuals. There was Louie, the French soldier, who became as a real son in the Grover Bullington family. We all laughed when he told Grover, "Mr. Bullington, you wear me out rising and sitting in the services."

We shall never forget George and Ellen Verity and her bravery when she learned that George was a member of the group made to participate in the infamous Death March to Bataan. It was months before she learned that he was alive. One of the greatest moments I have known came when I heard his voice from San Francisco speaking to us in Little Rock, asking us to meet them in the church at Wichita Falls and receive him into membership in the church.

A happy group stood at the altar one glorious afternoon and took again the sacred vows with George and thanked God that George and Ellen were together again to receive the blessings of the church. We have never known a more touching experience.

Mr. Bridwell gave up the chairmanship of the Board in the fall of 1941, soon after the death of his wife. The Board adopted a touching resolution praising Mrs. Bridwell and extending warm sympathy to him, after which the pastor led in prayer, and the meeting closed with singing, "Blest Be the Tie That Binds." The secretary recorded that in the history of the church there had never been such a Board meeting. "We were very near our Maker—and we felt His guidance, and His presence and His power more surely because of the service and inspiration of one man—Brother Bridwell."

THE PERKINS LECTURES

In 1942-43 Mr. and Mrs. J. J. Perkins established an endowment fund to provide a series of annual lectures in First Church to be called the Perkins Lectures. The committee to select the speakers were named to include representatives of the church, of the Perkins family, and Dr.

(Bishop) Martin, who has served as often as he could since leaving the church. Mrs. Perkins says that the lectureship was established at the suggestion of Dr. Martin.[5]

The first series were given February 28—March 5, 1943, by Dr. Roy L. Smith, editor of the *Christian Advocate*, on the topic "Becoming Spiritual Experts."

Outstanding preachers and scholars have made this series a memorable one for those who have heard them, and the lectures have certainly enriched the religious lives of the members of the church and others who have attended. The list of speakers reveals this richness:

Dr. Roy L. Smith, 1943; Bishop Edwin Holt Hughes, 1944; Dr. Norman Vincent Peale, 1945; Dr. G. Ray Jordan, 1947; Dr. Richard C. Raines, 1948; Bishop Paul E. Martin, 1949; Dr. John Sutherland Bonnell, 1950; Dr. George A. Buttrick, 1951; Dr. Elton Trueblood, 1952; Dr. Charles Ray Goff, 1953; Dr. Leslie D. Weatherhead, 1954; Dr. Paul Scherer, 1955; Dr. James S. Stewart, 1956; Bishop Gerald Kennedy, 1957; Dr. Robert J. McCracken, 1958; Dr. Perry E. Gresham, 1959; Dr. Ralph W. Sockman, 1960; Dr. James T. Cleland, 1961; Dr. Theodore Gill, 1962; Dr. Maldwyn Edwards, 1963; The Reverend A. P. Tremlett, 1964; Dr. Carlyle Marney, 1966; Dr. Harold Roberts, 1967; Dr. Albert Outler, 1968; Bishop Paul E. Martin, 1969; Dr. Browne Barr, 1970, Dr. Arthur Jackson, 1971, Dr. David H. C. Reed, 1972, and Dr. Robert J. Campbell, 1973.

It is appropriate that Bishop Martin delivered the lectures on two occasions—in 1949 and in 1969. He has commented on the significance of this lectureship:

The establishment in 1943 by Mr. and Mrs. J. J. Perkins of the Perkins Lectures marked an event unique in Methodism. A magnificent gift established a trust fund whereby an outstanding spiritual leader could be brought each year. The gift has paid large dividends in the life of the community and surrounding area. Renowned ministers throughout the United States, Great Britain, and Australia have delivered the Lectures. I am humbled by the thought that twice I have delivered the Lectures.

Appreciation for the lectures was felt by the members of the church, of course, and undoubtedly W. B. Hamilton represented them when he spoke to the Board of Stewards about the lectures following the first series, expressing his deep gratitude, personally and officially, for this new feature in the life of First Church.

The program of the church continued to grow and to attract the

members. "Our great sanctuary is filled each Sunday with sincere wor-
shippers," Dr. Martin told the Quarterly Conference on March 8, 1943.
"Our soldier's work has been commended by leading authorities in that
field." The church brought—or helped to bring—to the city such persons as Grace Sloan Overton and Russell Dicks for special addresses.

So popular had Dr. Martin become that the Quarterly Conference
petitioned Bishop Holt to return him "for the coming year, and per-
manently if he may." The resolution had a terse P.S. that said: "We
want our preacher back."

Great Church Music

One of the traditions for which Paul E. Martin is best remembered
at First Church is the Easter lily processional that he inaugurated. Miss
Edith Slaten, a choir member for sixty-five years, wrote about its origin
in these terms:

It came to pass that five months before the dedication of the temple in
Wichita Falls, Paul Martin became high priest. And he had a cherished dream
of a beautiful Easter service. He meditated upon it day and night. Where it
came from, he did not say; he only said it was not original with him. He
could see a long line of singers bearing lilies as gifts and placing them upon
the altar. . . . When he came to the temple and saw its pictured windows in
the morning sunlight, its high arches and cloistered aisles and heard the great
organ played by Nita [Akin] who is a master of the organ, and heard the
choir, he knew he had found what he sought.

He counseled with Pearl [Calhoun Davis] who instructed the singers
because she was skilful, with Nita, the organist, with Mary [Anthony] who
had charge of adorning the church with flowers each Sunday, and with
Elizabeth [Wright Berry] who instructed the children's choir, and they heard
him gladly, for there was nothing like the lily processional in all the land.
The people also brought their gifts to buy lilies in honor of the living and
the dead and to carry to the sick, the lame, and the halt after the service.

The older men of the choir were much disturbed. They said it was un-
seemly for them to carry lilies in the temple. One said he would have to pass
the seat of his friend, Bill, and Bill would laugh at him. But Pearl who was
both charming and wise would not be denied. "Wherefore should anyone
laugh?" she asked, "you are part of a picture." With this and other reason-
ings, she calmed the fearful ones and made up their minds.

When Easter was come, the singers were all of one accord in the temple.
None thought of himself or how he appeared before men. The temple was
filled with people. As the processional moved toward the altar, the faint odor
of lilies floated over the room, and when the lilies were in their places, the
beauty of the altar was like the benediction after prayer. The people loved

the processional and it became a tradition. The fame of it was noised abroad and many inquiries were made from far places by those who loved beauty. There was also an aged woman in the temple whose custom it was to rise and face the processional as it moved forward, and none laughed or made her afraid.

"He was always interested in and supportive of our music program at the church," testifies Mrs. J. W. Akin, Jr., accomplished organist at the church for many years. "He usually chose the hymns for the services. His support enabled us to provide a rich program of choral, instrumental, and congregational music during the years of his pastorate."[6]

Serving the Members and the Community

As was always true, the Martins made their parsonage home virtually an "open house" for all who would enter—and encouraged others to do likewise. Miss Llerena Friend, prominent Texas historian of Wichita Falls and Austin, says:

I was fortunate to be in First Church when Paul and Mildred Martin came there, and I loved them both dearly. . . . We were all devoted to them. Mildred was my Sunday School teacher. . . .

I remember how they made the parsonage a place of warmth and welcome to members of the Sunday School class and the Wesleyan Service Guild. Dr. Martin always seemed to have fun, even to the extent of modeling caps or hats or something we had for one occasion.

He was pastor when the war came, and even before December 7, the church had inaugurated a policy of welcome for the men at Sheppard Field, one that has continued to this day. . . . Old and young, married and unmarried took part in entertaining both the U.S. and foreign boys there—and still hear from them all over the world. I remember I was baking apricot pies at the church on December 7. We also had a night for games and square dancing. Some tut-tutting went on among the church members, but Dr. Martin figured that he had the boys in the church.

As this testimony indicates, Mrs. Martin shared equally in the universal affection and esteem in which the pastor was held. Mrs. Grover Bullington recalls that she frequently called Mrs. Martin "Sister Phoebe" after the New Testament church member who was famous for her role in serving others.

Near the end of Dr. Martin's pastorate his mother died (April 2, 1944), after several years of ill health, some spent in Wichita Falls where he and Mrs. Martin could look after her. She had gone back to Blossom, however, and it was there she died, and there she was buried.

Services were held by the Blossom pastor, Rev. M. C. Sooter, Rev. E. A. Hunter, district superintendent at Wichita Falls, Rev. Paul C. Stephenson, pastor at Floral Heights Church in Wichita Falls and a longtime friend, and the faithful family friend, Rev. J. D. Thomas.

Dr. Martin gave much credit to the fine cooperation given him by able staff members in the persons of Rev. Dan R. Robinson, Rev. Earl R. Hoggard, and Rev. and Mrs. Merlin Merrill. He often paid tribute to "dedicated and loyal secretaries" who served him, including Miss Marguerite Haynie, Miss Mary Ward, Mrs. Walter Armstrong, and Mrs. Russel Moxley.

A Broader and Deeper Ministry

Dr. Martin was invited with increasing frequency to speak and preach outside the city. He was the "conference preacher" at both the East Oklahoma and the West Oklahoma conferences, preached at Eastland and at the Bloys Camp Meeting in West Texas for a series of services, taught in a leadership school at Electra, and gave the baccalaureate sermon at McMurry College, Abilene. At a Board of Stewards meeting after the 1944 General Conference, Mr. Perkins was openly talking about the possibilities that Dr. Martin might be elected bishop.

Looking back in his "Reflections" on his years as pastor of First Church, Wichita Falls, Bishop Martin recalls some of the highlights in events and some of the highlights in personal relationships in Wichita Falls.

"He identified himself in his ministry with all areas of church life—preaching, worship, evangelism, service, personal faith, music, counseling, education, and stewardship," recalls Dr. Earl R. Hoggard, who served as associate pastor with Dr. Martin for almost the entire six years.

He was equally concerned with each of these areas.

Another important part of his ministry was in visitation. He and Mrs. Martin spent unnumbered hours in visiting for the church—both members and prospects. They worked together as a team, coordinated and trained, with both of them familiar with the elements that make up a helpful ministry. Dr. Martin missed very few balls, but if he missed one, Mildred caught it on the first bounce and handed it back to him. We averaged adding 300 persons each year to church membership during those five years.

Still a different contribution he made was to enlarge the sense of unity in the congregation. As in any church there were diverse elements and loyalties. He focused the concern of the membership on the larger goals of the Christian life.[7]

All of this meant that the Martins provided a very warm, personalized fellowship for the members and constituents of the church. They made many persons feel that they had a special closeness to the Martins. Even now, after nearly thirty years, many of the members of the church reveal that they feel this special sense of fellowship. Each person was made to feel important to them: "Everybody is Somebody," as one of his sermon topics declared.

"Paul E. Martin developed significantly as a preacher while in Wichita Falls," continues Dr. Hoggard.

I heard him preach morning and evening almost every Sunday for five years. He worked hard at being all that a pastor ought to be to a church, and a part of that was his sermon preparation. He set aside time every week for study and sermon creation. Every time I heard him speak publicly—at the church or elsewhere—it was obvious that he had made special preparation for that particular message.

Part of Dr. Martin's growth in his preaching was undoubtedly due to the support of a congregation that was appreciative and that called forth his best. A congregation can influence its pastor's preaching—for good or ill. The messages that he brought were in terms of a balanced, vital, growing faith that did not promise comfort or any easy happiness but that provided challenges, hopes, and high goals, presented as an exciting and satisfying way of life.

Dr. Martin had the ability to present great tasks appealingly to members of the congregation—individually and collectively. He found in the congregation a number of persons who had already responded to great causes with their support. Dr. Martin encouraged these persons to continue and to enlarge such support. He was also able to suggest new channels for advancing the work of the Kingdom and of the church. The establishment of the Perkins Lectures was one example of this.

The years at First Church, Wichita Falls, thus were a time for a rich ministry, with Paul E. Martin as pastor and with a loyal and generous congregation of lay persons committed to giving themselves in service to the city—and to the world. Dr. Martin showed himself a master builder in his years there. He led in creating a deeper spirit of dedication and unity among the members, and he helped build a greater sense of community and world responsibility among the leaders of the city, both within and without the church he served.

CHAPTER SIX

"Consecrated—for the Office And Work of a Bishop"

"NO ONE IS MORE of what a bishop should be than Paul Martin," declared Bishop A. Frank Smith on November 4, 1960, at a meeting of the Board of Trustees of Southern Methodist University.[1] What factors led to his being elected bishop? What were the discernible developments in his personality and his ministerial career after election? What style of episcopal ministry did he assume?

We have noted the steady development in Dr. Martin's preaching and pastoral qualities. At the same time he was developing in certain other ways that might be called qualities of churchmanship. These included his service beyond the local church or district, chiefly to the annual conference, but also outside it.

We have seen examples in previous chapters of this wider influence. From 1930 to 1934 he was recording secretary of the Conference Board of Education. He was continued as a member of that board in the 1934-38 quadrennium, but when made presiding elder in 1935 he was automatically dropped from all board memberships by a standing rule of the conference. In 1934 the Conference named him a trustee of Southern Methodist University, a position he held until his retirement in 1968.

In 1940 he returned to membership on the Conference Board of Education and was elected president for the quadrennium. He gave helpful leadership to the Board, assisted by the Rev. Paul O. Cardwell as vice-president and the Rev. G. Henry Mood as recording secretary. The Rev. Ira C. Kiker was the executive secretary at that time. The conference board was unique in that it also had on it three conference members who were staff members of the General Board of Education: the Rev. Walter Towner, the Rev. O. W. Moerner, and the Rev. Walter N. Vernon. Other members of that board who have served the church significantly include the Rev. Durwood Fleming, now president of Southwestern University, the Rev. Joe Brown Love, Dr. L. F. Sensabaugh, Dr. Marshall T. Steel, and Estelle Blanton Barber.

In 1942 Dr. Martin presented Mr. and Mrs. J. J. Perkins, members of the church he served, to the conference on the occasion on which they presented a fund of $100,000 to be used by the Board of Pensions to increase pensions for retired members of the conference.

Neutrality in Conference Struggle

The early thirties was a time of turbulent relationships in the North Texas Conference. The situation was so unhappy that Dr. Martin gave some thought to the possibility of transferring to another conference.

The two factions involved, on one side, such persons as Harry G. Ryan, S. A. Barnes, Harold G. Cooke, Sam M. Black, and J. H. Groseclose; and on the other, Bishop H. A. Boaz, Frank M. Richardson, and Charles C. Selecman. The issues were complex but included personal relationships, struggle for place and power, and the depression with its financial crises in pastor's salaries.

The situation resulted in two of the most heated and bitter sessions ever held on the conference floor—at Bonham in 1931, and at Gainsville in 1932. It affected membership on conference boards and agencies, the election of General Conference delegates, and the making of appointments; and it involved the transfer of ministers to other conferences in an effort to clear up the situation.[2]

Bishop Martin has summarized his position at that time in this manner:

Though strong pressure was made for the support of one side or the other I could not accept the tactics employed by certain parties, and I was resolved not to be embroiled in the dispute. I was determined not to allow envy and jealousy toward a brother preacher to dominate my life. I was convinced then, as I am now, that it was an empty honor to be elected to any high office through political maneuvering. For a minister to possess the lasting satisfaction of being true to his holy calling, he must live on a higher plane.

ELECTION TO GENERAL CONFERENCE

Perhaps because of his efforts to avoid taking sides in the conference dispute, Dr. Martin was elected on the first ballot—thus to head the delegation—to the General Conference of 1938. It was an unusual thing for a person to head a delegation the first time elected, but this revealed his high standing among his fellow ministers. Two of his fellow delegates were elected bishops at the 1938 Conference in Birmingham—Drs. Charles C. Selecman and William C. Martin. Dr. Paul Martin also headed the delegation to the Uniting Conference in 1939. He calls the year of 1938 a "red letter year" because of these historic conferences. He writes:

I led the clerical delegation from the North Texas Conference to the final session of the Methodist Episcopal Church, South, in the spring, and in the fall was elected to be the leader to the historic Unification Conference in Kansas City. The date of April 29, 1939, when the three Methodisms were combined, has a place in history along with the date of John Wesley's spiritual rebirth on May 24, 1738, and Christmas, 1784, when American Methodism was organized at Lovely Lane Chapel in Baltimore, Maryland.

At the General Conference in 1938, Charles C. Selecman and William C. Martin, of our delegation, were elected to the episcopacy, and Will Martin honored me by selecting me as one of the two elders to escort him to the altar and lay my hands on his head in the service of consecration. Six years later he laid his hands on my head in a similar service. The friendship with Bishop Selecman is a blessed memory; the fellowship with Bishop Martin[3] is a continuing inspiration.

At the General Conference of 1940, Dr. Paul Martin was again a delegate, with the delegation headed by Dr. Umphrey Lee, President of Southern Methodist University. He was also a delegate to the 1940 Jurisdictional Conference. This was where bishops were thereafter elected, but the conference decided to elect no bishops at that session.

Back in 1938 at the General Conference at Birmingham, Alabama, Dr. Paul Martin had received a few votes for bishop on the first ballot, on which his longtime friend Dr. Ivan Lee Holt had been elected bishop. Dr. W. Angie Smith, pastor-host to the conference, had received a rather strong vote from 119 supporters, but this support had gradually yielded.

Between 1940 and 1944, Dr. Martin was more and more receiving public recognition in the Jurisdiction. Southwestern University had already conferred on him the honorary degree of Doctor of Divinity "in its desire to recognize outstanding achievement in behalf of humanity." He preached the baccalaureate sermon at McMurry College in June, 1943, and in October, 1943, he preached at both the East Oklahoma and the West Oklahoma Conferences.

THE ELECTION OF 1944

Dr. W. Angie Smith headed the North Texas delegation to the 1944 General Conference and Jurisdictional Conference. Dr. Smith, as we have noted, had substantial support for the office of bishop at the 1938 conference in Birmingham of the former Southern Church. It was expected that when the South Central Jurisdictional Conference met in Tulsa in June, 1944, he would be at or near the top in the voting. Others who were expected to be high in the voting were Dr. Paul W. Quillian of Houston and Dr. Charles E. Schofield. Dr. Schofield represented the former Methodist Episcopal Church constituency, and this group had high hopes of electing one of their number as one of the new bishops. Speculation regarding the election of bishops made mention of Paul Martin's qualities, but it was considered that if Dr. W. Angie Smith were elected, it would be unlikely that another minister from the same conference would be chosen.

When the voting began in Boston Avenue Methodist Church in Tulsa, 175 votes were needed for election. This number remained fairly consistent throughout the series of eleven ballots that were carried through in the election of the two bishops that were chosen. On Ballot One, W. Angie Smith received 148 votes, Charles E. Schofield, 63; Paul W. Quillian, 62; Edmund Heinsohn of Austin, 38; Umphrey Lee of Dallas, 36; John N. R. Score of Fort Worth, 36; and Paul E. Martin, 35.

On Ballot Two, W. Angie Smith was elected with 200 votes, and Quillian with 81 votes was ahead of Schofield with 75. Heinsohn had received 46 votes, Lee 32, and Martin 29. Ballot Three saw Quillian's votes move ahead to 95, while Schofield's increase reached 79. Martin had been moved to third place in the voting although he received only 27 votes, for Heinsohn had received 24 and Score 20. Ballots Four, Five, and Six held at about the same standings, with Quillian supporters holding their lead but never going over 110 in number of votes. Schofield remained steadily second, the number of votes for him reaching as many as 102, while the number of Martin voters had slowly increased to 40.

After a ten-minute recess at midmorning on June 14, a remarkable Ballot Seven resulted in an almost even tie between the three: Schofield 81; Martin, 80; Quillian, 78. On Ballot Eight, a considerable number of Quillian supporters evidently swung to Martin, for this time he received 104 votes to 37 for Quillian, but with 79 of Schofield's supporters holding fast in their loyalty to him.

On Ballots Nine, Ten, and Eleven the move toward Martin continued, with 135, 152, and 170 votes, and with Quillian's supporters yielding more and more, but with Schofield's supporters holding firm with never fewer than 70 votes being cast in his favor. On Ballot Eleven, however, 170 votes were sufficient to elect, and Paul E. Martin with 178 had been elected a bishop in the Methodist church. "The greatest thing I ever saw him do," says Dr. Harry Denman, beloved lay preacher of the church at large, "was when he was elected bishop: He simply sat still in his seat for some moments, quietly."

During the early voting friends of Paul Martin were mildly hopeful that the voting would turn to him. Among the most active supporters of Dr. Martin was his great lay friend of Wichita Falls, Mr. Joe J. Perkins, who headed the lay delegation from North Texas Conference. As the votes increased for Dr. Martin, Mr. Perkins renewed his efforts of persuasion among the delegates. "Paul Martin had every qualification in the world" (for being elected bishop), said Bishop A. Frank Smith. But the specific credit for his election, so far as human effort was concerned, goes to this good friend, Mr. Perkins, continued Bishop Smith.[4]

Following his election, he was appropriately escorted to the platform by Bishop Ivan Lee Holt, longtime friend and onetime teacher, and Mr. Perkins. Bishop A. Frank Smith pointed out that the conference broke precedent in having Mr. Perkins help escort Paul Martin to the front after his election; it had always been done before by two bishops. "There is no law against it," said Bishop Smith, "and it meant much more to Mr. Perkins than it would to anybody else." Bishop Smith related that he later said to Mr. Perkins: "Brother Joe, I never saw any man trying as hard in the world to kick his preacher out, but you were kicking him upstairs."[5]

Judge Leslie J. Lyons of Kansas City secured the floor after the election and read the lines that had been penned from the Missouri Conference, called "The Bishops Grow—Deep in the Heart of Texas," found at the beginning of this volume.

In a press conference held shortly after the election, Mrs. Martin put her arm around the shoulder of Walter N. Vernon, editor of the *Daily Advocate* and himself a onetime Blossom resident, saying, "Walter, did you ever think that a little girl like me from the cotton fields of Blossom would ever be a Bishop's wife?"

Her sense of humor had already showed up during the election. As the voting started shifting toward Dr. Martin there occurred one of those classic incidents that have become a part of the folklore of the jurisdiction. Several delegates from one of the northern conferences were concerned to know how Dr. Martin stood on the use of tobacco. They sought out Mrs. Martin and hesitantly asked her how her husband felt about smoking. They were assured he was against the use of tobacco, especially by preachers. Feeling satisfied, they started to leave, when Mrs. Martin called out, "Just a minute. I think in all fairness I should tell you that I dip snuff!" The startled delegates looked at her open-eyed for a minute, then chuckled and said, "Sister, you'll do."

The service of consecration was held in the sanctuary of First Methodist Church in Tulsa. Bishop John M. Moore gave the consecration sermon. Two close friends were chosen by Bishop-elect Martin to add their hands to those of the bishops in the consecration: the Rev. Paul C. Stephenson and the Rev. Wesley V. Hite.

Splendid and Miserable

What did this election mean to the Martins' way of life? Gilbert Highet has said, commenting on a book about Igor Stravinski:

It is both splendid and miserable to be world famous. If you are, you get the best seats in the theatre, and the finest suite in the hotel, and top priority in air travel. Seldom do you have to worry about money. Secretaries, companions, servants are eager to work for you. You get lots of affection, and (unlike ordinary people) you seldom doubt the value of your own existence. But for all this you must pay a hard price . . . You have no private life, unless you devote an inordinate amount of time and energy to safeguarding it. All your natural weaknesses are exposed and magnified. You are harassed by photographers and caricatured by cartoonists and misrepresented by enemies and parodied by clowns. Whenever I read the biography of a much admired man or woman, I always pay special attention to these splendors and miseries."[6]

Obviously, Bishop and Mrs. Martin have not been subjected to *all*

these "miseries," nor had all these "splendors" thrust upon them. Perhaps
their experience is best described in the bishop's own words:

The election to the episcopacy brought about a complete change in our
lives. We left a wonderful pastorate of one of the most beautiful churches of
Methodism where we had an attractive and comfortable home and were surrounded by gifted and thoughtful members to go to two other states in which
no bishop had resided for years and where no home waited for our occupancy.
The war was on and the city in which we were to reside (Little Rock) was
filled with army officers and few homes were available. Instead of preaching
twice each Sunday to the same people I was to occupy many pulpits, and to
fill such assignments I was to travel long distances each month.

But the Arkansas-Louisiana Methodists opened their arms and their
hearts to their new bishop and his wife, and when they left sixteen years
later Dr. C. M. Reeves was to write them:

In your own dear Texas they can—and doubtless will—give you costly
expressions of their love and appreciation, but they can never give you there
or anywhere else more genuine offerings of love and devotion than are
symbolized by the "black-gum snuff sticks" with which you were greeted on
your arrival in Arkansas in June of 1944!"[7]

LEAVE-TAKING AT WICHITA FALLS

But before the move to Little Rock came the leave-taking at Wichita
Falls. The people of First Church were rightly proud of the recognition
that had come to their pastor, but at the same time woeful because he
must now leave them. People outside their own church and denomination shared this sense of both pride and loss. A great interdenominational
service was held on Sunday evening, June 25, with major churches in
the city dismissing their own services to join the crowd at First Methodist. A quarter-page section in the *Wichita Falls Record News* announced
the event. It was sponsored by First Christian Church, First Baptist
Church, First Presbyterian Church, Church of the Good Shepherd, Floral
Heights Methodist Church, Highland Heights Christian Church, Lamar
Avenue Baptist Church, and Grace Methodist Church, all of which
joined with First Methodist for this occasion. Dr. E. A. Hunter, district
superintendent, presided at the service, and Dr. Paul C. Stephenson of
Floral Heights Church, because of his close friendship with the Martins
since seminary days, represented many other close friends and fellow
Methodists.

On a less formal basis was a great reception to which 3,000 people came on the lawn of the home of Mr. and Mrs. J. J. Perkins, for which Mrs. C. W. Snider served as general chairman. The church bulletin for June 18 said, "Proudly, but with tears in our hearts, we surrender to the church at large the unselfish devotion, consecrated leadership, and human kindliness of Paul and Mildred Martin."

The Board of Stewards at a meeting on October 2 adopted a Special Resolution that expressed, as nearly as words can, their deep feeling about the Martins:

To the world let us say of Paul Martin that he is the best. He is a builder of churches, a preacher of sermons, a practitioner of love, a transformer of lives. He is a man of God—such intellectual faculties, such grace, such dignity, such understanding and love of mankind, such spiritual influence; surely the Divine waved his magic wand when he was born.

. . . He is a scholar but not bookish; an orator but not superficial; a genuine Christian but not a narrow fanatic. . . . He stands like a king among us but always with the common touch. . . . He never engages in caustic arguments; he just tells the truth and goes his way. . . .

We never saw Paul Martin frantic; we never saw him maddened. . . .

Paul had no dreams of power, no ambitions for the glitter and glow of rank. . . . His true eloquence is found in the magic of his good life.

Honors have been thrust upon him and he has always been kind and gracious, but after these things he never sought. . . . So to this lad born under a Texas sun, with warm heart and tender ministry, we officially pay humble and immortal tribute. . . .

To Mrs. Martin let us say, we hold you in holy bonds of love and spiritual esteem. . . . Here is a lady of Christian character and strength to match the greatness of Paul in every way.

Though the Martins were separated by space from the people of Wichita Falls following their move, close ties still bound them to many in the church there. From time to time, there have been return visits—to preach, to lecture, to marry, to comfort the bereaved, to administer the vows of church membership, to enjoy the depths of Christian fellowship.

CHAPTER SEVEN

In the Council of Bishops

IN THE COUNCIL OF BISHOPS the newer members were usually more seen than heard. Gradually, however, Paul E. Martin moved more and more into a position of leadership in the Council; perhaps the peak of recognition came with his election to serve as president of the body for the year 1961-62.

The meetings of the Council were occasions not only for the consideration of certain matters of business for which the bishops were responsible, but also for the deepening of Christian fellowship and for the broadening of horizons of Christian perspective and concerns.

For example, at the meeting on April 24, 1944, just before Paul E. Martin became a member of the group, Bishop Charles C. Selecman led a devotional service in observance of the assembling on that day in San Francisco of the United Nations Conference on International Organization. Prayer was offered for the United Nations Conference, for our country, our allies, and our enemies; for Europe, Asia, Africa, and Latin America; and for worldwide Methodism.[1]

In December, 1948, Bishop Martin was leader of a service of worship at a session devoted to the orientation of newly elected bishops. Later that year he joined other bishops in issuing a statement challenging some of the allegations made by the House Committee on UnAmerican Activities: "We expressly deny that Communism has infiltrated our Protestant churches." At another meeting he was named to a special committee to study the feasibility of proposing a Central (national) Methodist Headquarters, and to the standing committee on Law and Administration.

FACING CONTEMPORARY IDEOLOGIES

A year later he participated in a rich program in the Council dealing with Contemporary Ideologies. An outstanding list of speakers brought fresh insights to the group: Sidney Hook, Sherwood Eddy, Louis Fischer, John C. Bennett, Mathew Spinka, Reinhold Niebuhr, Norman Thomas, Max Lerner, and Pitirim A. Sorokin. It is doubtful that many other groups in the nation could have brought together at one time a more impressive panel of experts than these notables.

In the Spring 1949 meeting the bishops faced a small but significant issue—what to do about a practice that had emerged of district superintendents (and even one bishop!) advertising in the *Christian Advocate* for ministers to fill certain pulpits. The practice was confined to Kansas, South Dakota, and Michigan. The conclusion of the Council's deliberation: "We feel that such action is not in harmony with the spirit of the itinerant system."

Bishop Martin agreed in the fall of 1950 to cooperate in a nationwide introduction of the new Revised Standard Version of the New Testament. The plan called for simultaneous public meetings in three thousand communities across the land on Tuesday, September 30, 1952, at which the new version would be introduced to the world. Bishop Martin agreed to serve on the Speakers' Bureau for the project.

There were lighter moments in the Council, of course. In December, 1950, Bishop Gerald Kennedy announced that he was sending a box of apples from his area to each of his fellow bishops. He dryly commented to his colleagues, "Like the apple in the Garden, they may not make us better but they may make us wiser." The use of humor in speaking and in dealing with persons was considered important enough that in one of the orientation sessions for new bishops in the Fall 1952 meeting, Bishop Donald H. Tippett made a presentation entitled "The Bishop and Humor." He pointed out that there are many different types of humor, ranging from caustic wit to kindly side-glances at the eccentricities of human nature. It was this latter type of humor at which Bishop Martin was truly a past master, and of which he made use from time to time.

Moral Issues

The Council frequently took positions on public issues that had moral implications. It publicly opposed sending a U.S. Ambassador to the Vatican and approved a bill to eliminate liquor advertising from radio and television airways. In April, 1952, Bishop Martin helped Dr. J. Q. Schisler of the General Board of Education (and a member of the North Arkansas Conference) to secure time to speak to the Council about the need for an emphasis on youth work for the coming quadrennium. Bishop Martin also served as chairman of a special committee in 1953 that smoothed out a misunderstanding regarding the attendance of a visiting bishop in India.

At the meeting of the Council in December, 1953, Bishop Martin reported officially on his Episcopal Visitation to Latin America. Elsewhere in this volume he relates some aspects of that trip. In his official report he emphasized the significance of Methodist schools in Latin America, pointing out, for instance, that one of them, the American Institute in Lins, was the largest school of any type in the city, and that it had recently been given by the city a site for a new school of dentistry. He called attention to the fact that in Porto Alegre, Brazil, where we have had a school for many years, the head of the Chamber of Commerce, the head of the State Police, and the treasurer of the state at that time were all Methodists. He closed his report by proposing that the time might have come for the Methodists to build a church in Latin America, and not simply service organizations, as important as these may be.

Opposing McCarthyism

At the same session he joined with other bishops in opposing the McCarthyism that was a public issue at that time. "We resent unproven assertions that the Protestant ministry is honeycombed with disloyalty. We are unalterably opposed to Communism, but we know that the alternative to Communism is not an American brand of fascism," they jointly declared.

During this session Bishop Martin was selected by ballot to serve as the fraternal delegate to the forthcoming General Conference of the Christian Methodist Episcopal Church. We have already noted his fraternal relationship with a C.M.E. Church in Wichita Falls.

In April, 1954, when the Council met in New York, Bishop Martin participated in several sessions held at the United Nations where addresses were given by several of the top members of the Secretariat, such as Benjamin Cohen, Andrew Cordier, and Ralph Bunche, and there was a welcoming statement from the secretary-general himself—Dag Hammer-skjold.

In November, 1954, Bishop Martin joined other bishops in adopting a statement from the Council declaring that "the historic decision of the Supreme Court abolishing segregation in the public school system is in keeping with the attitude of The Methodist Church, . . . but the ultimate success of the ruling will be determined in the hearts of the people of the nation." The bishops of the Southeastern Jurisdiction went on record as feeling it would be better that no statement be issued at that time.

As the church moved closer and closer to the time of abolishing the Central (Negro) Jurisdiction, Bishop Martin was among those who were to have a crucial role to play. Some instances of the early facing of these issues occurred in the Council of Bishops, where quite naturally the black and the white bishops worked side by side. In April, 1955, Bishop Martin was present when the bishops of the Central Jurisdiction and of the two southern jurisdictions met during the Council sessions to "consider to-gether the issues that lie in the question of integration' and other related matters."

Memoirs for Colleagues

It was also in that April meeting that Bishop Martin was asked to present a memoir for Bishop Hoyt M. Dobbs, a friend of his from semi-nary days. In addition, Bishop Dobbs had lived in retirement—and in ill health—within the bounds of the Arkansas-Louisiana Area served by Bishop Martin for a number of years. The younger bishop had frequently visited the older one, and in the memoir paid a high tribute to Hoyt Dobbs's deeply-ingrained and never-failing graciousness and courtesy to-ward everyone he met. Paul Martin told of one personal experience that illustrated his appreciation for this trait in his dear friend:

He called me "Paul" until I was elected bishop, and from that time on he never addressed me as anything but "Bishop." On one occasion I said to him, "Bishop Dobbs, you know we have known each other for a long time. I knew you in S.M.U." And he said, "Yes, Yes." I went on, "And you have always called me Paul." Again he agreed, "Yes, Yes." I continued, "We have had you in our home." To his "Yes, Yes" of assent, I went on, "Up until the time I became a bishop you called me Paul; but you have never called me

Paul since that time. I wish, Bishop Dobbs, that you would still call me Paul."
And in that characteristic fashion he responded, "Yes, Bishop." And that was
that!

On the occasion of the 250th anniversary year of Charles Wesley's
birth, Bishop Martin delighted the entire Council with a devotional message on Charles Wesley as a hymn writer. It was titled, "The Singer Makes
the Song," and is an excellent though brief analysis of the place of hymn-
ody in the life of the church, as well as of Charles Wesley's gifts as
composer and poet.

ISSUES OF INTEGRATION

The issue of segregation and the church's position on it kept coming
to the Council. At the December, 1956 meeting, a copy of a letter was
read from a person in Washington, D.C. (whether or not a Methodist is
not revealed) written to Pope Pius XII which contained the following:

On other occasions I have written you, but received no answer. Without
a doubt my letter fell into the hands of Pharisees within your own household
who no doubt considered me a fool for having written you. Such hypocrites
are beneath contempt. . . . I beg your best consideration in directing your
clergymen to make an all-out effort to influence American Christians to give
up segregation . . . against the Negro, who is a child of God the same as
a white human being.

At the same meeting another letter came from Mississippi—just across
the river from Bishop Martin's Louisiana Conference—protesting that
"the continued and persistent publication of literature, articles, and photo-
graphs in our church literature praising integration of the white and
colored races in our churches is offensive, unwarranted, and wholly un-
necessary."

AFRICAN VISITATION

A report on his visitation to Africa was on the docket of the Council
meeting in November, 1957. Among other things, Bishop Martin reported that he found a church in South Africa "with a warped attitude
toward Humanity. . . . [revealed by] the height of white arrogance and
the depth of white fear." He praised the work of Methodist and other
Christian missions and quoted a hymn by Hosea K. Nyanbanga used at a
service he attended at the Methodist school in Mrewa in Southern
Rhodesia:

Give a thought to Africa
　'Neath the burning sun.
Hosts of weary hearts are there
　Waiting to be won.
Many idols have they
　But from swamp and clod
Many a voice is crying out
　for the living God.

One of the high positions to which he was elected by his fellow bishops was membership on the Council on World Service and Finance. This choice was made by ballot at a Council meeting during the General Conference of 1960, and he was elected on the first ballot taken. But the highest position to which the Council had the power to elect was its own presidency, and that honor came to him at the same meeting. Actually, he was first elected President-Designate in 1960 to serve for the 1961-62 term.

In the Spring 1960 meeting he gave the memoir for Bishop H. Bascom Watts, praising him as "a great interpreter of the Gospel." Four years later he performed a similar service for Mrs. A. Frank Smith, whom he had known almost all his life. He mentioned that for years, as Bishop Smith had traveled across the nation, he had written his wife every day. "Through the years," Bishop Martin said, "she and her husband served as ideals for us."

When the Council met in Boston in April, 1961, a petition was presented to it from 181 students at Boston University School of Theology, urging the bishops to encourage the seminaries in the South to open their doors to all races. "We feel," the petition read, "that most students and faculty leaders would welcome and assist such action at this time." Bishop Martin could take satisfaction in the fact that Perkins School of Theology, of whose Trustees' Committee he was chairman, had taken this step some years earlier.

PRESIDENT OF THE COUNCIL

The twelve-month term in which Bishop Martin served as president of the Council was undoubtedly one of the high points of his career. Two meetings were involved—one at Gatlinburg, Tennessee, November 14-16, 1961, and the other at Mexico City, April 24-27, 1962. The Message from the Bishops at the fall meeting declared:

The making of peace is our business, our sacred trust. . . . We commend our fellow-Methodists for their common sense and loyalty in resisting continuous and insidious attacks upon the church and church leaders under the guise of patriotism and anti-communism by self-appointed, irresponsible persons and groups. . . . Outwardly we [as the American people] are very religious. Our worship, however, is of the lips, not of the heart. We . . . obey our own desires, not God's loves. . . . We need to repent of our sins and return to God.

Following the meeting, Bishop Martin, as president of the Council, wrote the Portugese Embassy in Washington, conveying the protest of the Council regarding the arrest and imprisonment of Methodist missionaries in Angola. A reply, in essence rejecting the protest, came back addressed to "Mr. Paul E. Martin, Bishop."

The meeting in Mexico City was unique in that it was the first—and only—meeting of the Council ever held outside the United States. The Bishop had arranged for the Council meetings to be held in the Reforma Hotel. He preached on Easter Sunday in Mexico City's Methodist "Cathedral"—Gante Church—in the heart of the capital city.

For the program features he had arranged two presentations on the task of appointment-making, one by Bishop Lloyd C. Wicke and the other by Bishop Marvin Franklin; and he planned another presentation by Bishop Nolan B. Harmon, Jr. on more general aspects of the work of the bishop.

Bishop Harmon, in closing his message, suggested to his colleagues:

Let us not forget that we have solemnly taken a vow that we will "faithfully exercise ourselves in the Holy Scriptures, that we will call upon God through study and prayer for a proper understanding of these; that we will show ourselves in all things an example of good works unto others, for the honor and glory of God." For myself, brethren, I like to read over every once in a while the vows I once took.

Bishop Martin could take satisfaction in having provided a significant session for the Council, and for setting the stage for all those present to rethink the commitment made when they took the vows of consecration. He continued his activity in the Council until retirement, and still attends the meetings when possible.

The Council of Bishops, by its very nature, develops some of the characteristics of a family. There certainly is created a closely knit fellowship between its members. Paul E. Martin was enriched by the fellowship he shared there for the years following 1944, and he, in turn, contributed to the feeling of warmth and high devotion among these "chief pastors."

CHAPTER EIGHT

Serving the Arkansas-Louisiana Area

THE FIRST EPISCOPAL ASSIGNMENT for Bishop Martin was the Arkansas-Louisiana Area; his residence was in Little Rock. He was welcomed by the Methodists of the two states. He was at the halfway point in his active ministry; he was still less than fifty years old, and he had brought to the assignment the experience of a successful pastor and presiding elder.

The two states had not been consistently joined together as an area. In recent times, in fact, they had been together only in 1930-34 when Bishop Hoyt M. Dobbs served both states while he was living in Shreveport. Before 1944, Arkansas had been linked sometimes with Oklahoma, sometimes with Missouri. Louisiana had been joined with the Houston Area, after Bishop Dobbs's tenure of eight years.

The two states had also had intermittent episcopal residency. When Bishop Hiram A. Boaz was assigned to the conference in Arkansas and Oklahoma for 1926-30, he became the first bishop to make Little Rock his home.[1] From 1930 to 1938 Bishop Dobbs lived in Shreveport, serving Louisiana all that time, but serving Arkansas only the first quadrennium. Bishop John M. Moore supervised the Arkansas and Missouri Conferences in 1934-38, and lived in Dallas; Bishop Charles C. Selecman had the Arkansas and Oklahoma Conferences in 1938-44 and lived in Oklahoma. From 1938 to 1944 Louisiana Methodism was attached to the Houston Area and served by Bishop A. Frank Smith. Thus the prospect of some years (sixteen, as it turned out) in the same area with the same bishop appealed to the Methodists of the two states.

METHODISM IN ARKANSAS AND LOUISIANA

Arkansas and Louisiana Methodism was older than the Texas Methodism that Bishop Martin knew so well. In fact, the two older states served as the gateway to Texas in the early years. The first Methodist work in Texas was carried on by Arkansas Methodist preachers along the Red River in what are now Red River and Bowie counties by such persons as William Stevenson (founder of Arkansas Methodism), Henry Stephenson, and John B. Denton. A few years later Henry Stephenson, James Stevenson, and others from Arkansas and Louisiana carried the gospel into East Texas.

There has been much crossing of Arkansas and Texas state lines by Methodist leaders, some of these being William C. Martin, Paul W. Quillian, Paul C. Stephenson, Francis A. Buddin, Marshall T. Steel, and J. N. R. Score, all of whom were close friends of Bishop Martin.

Methodism in the two states had been improving since the era (1896-97) during which Bishop Eugene R. Hendrix wrote:

Returned . . . from my fall conferences in Texas, Mississippi, and Louisiana where I greatly enjoyed friendship with my brethren, seeking to save them from over-profession and arrested development. . . .

At home after holding three conferences in Arkansas. . . . Many changes rendered necessary by brethren having too little resources for the pastorate. . . . A type of religious fanaticism in the White River Conference needed to be checked by the presentation of the whole gospel.[2]

When Bishop John M. Moore served Arkansas in 1934-38 he commented on "the progressive spirit" that permeated both conferences, and noted that

they were ready for forward movements. J. Q. Schisler, Secretary of Sunday Schools, and A. W. Wasson, Secretary of Foreign Missions, were in the group and leading. The presiding elders were alert and vigorous leaders of the preachers and their district. . . . With heroism and determination it [the depression] was faithfully faced and Methodism won.[3]

As Bishop Martin took up the guidance of the area he found a number of problems in Arkansas and Louisiana requiring solution, according to Bishop Aubrey G. Walton, then a pastor in Arkansas. "There were wounds which needed healing. There were divisions which required elimination. There were misunderstandings and friction within the Church in both states."[4]

GETTING ACQUAINTED

Bishop and Mrs. Martin began at once to seek to meet the needs of the area. They started in a way they considered basic to their style of ministry: to become acquainted with the ministers and laymen of the area. He (and usually she was with him) visited every one of the twenty-two districts. In every town he visited he went to the parsonage to get acquainted with the parsonage family. He ruefully admits that in Louisiana on every visit he was served the state's typically strong coffee—until he found he "couldn't take it," and had to decline the offers!

The capacity to remember persons and their names was a great asset to the Martins. One Louisiana minister, the Rev. Jolly B. Harper, reflects this feeling:

Bishop Martin is the first Bishop I ever really knew. He was the first to cross the threshold of my home, the first to eat a meal in my home, the first to preach in my church. He was the first ever to know me wherever he met me. His predecessors, all fine gentlemen, knew me when I gave my name. I never failed to say, "This is Jolly Harper."

A very short time after I first met Bishop Martin, he came back in the interest of the great Crusade for Christ. After he had spoken, I went to shake his hand, and he immediately said, "Hello, Jolly." This was the first time any bishop had ever recognized me and called me by my first name.[5]

One of the earliest meetings the Martins attended involved an outdoor picnic lunch. Mrs. Martin had not been publicly introduced when mealtime arrived. During the lunch she spotted an older man, Brother Dunn, eating alone, so she went over and visited with him. She brought him some additional food and had a nice visit. Later he learned that she was the bishop's wife, and at first he did not believe it. "You mean," he said, "that this woman with lipstick and wearing a pretty red dress is the bishop's wife?" When assured that this was true, he said, "Well, I still like her."

Rev. E. Clifton Rule writes:

Time after time, when we had a big Methodist gathering we would find that Mrs. Martin had gone out of her way to find some persons who were not receiving much attention. She would have introduced herself and have gotten into a good conversation with them. Often, when circumstances permitted, she would ask them to come up and meet the bishop.[6]

The new bishop's first annual conference session was that of North Arkansas, meeting in Morrillton. As he met with the district superintendents in the cabinet, he showed great concern for careful appointment-making, and one of the group, Sam B. Wiggins, wrote: "He presided like a veteran." Mr. Wiggins was instructed by the cabinet to write representatives of the cabinet in the other conferences, assuring them of their good impression of the new bishop.

One district superintendent in the early period of Bishop Martin's tenure in North Arkansas, Dr. Ira A. Brumley, reports on appointment-making:

We had some ministers who were hard to place but he gave every consideration to them, and did the best he could for them. We spent about as much time placing these few men as in the placing of the remainder of the total group.

One morning he called the cabinet out of the conference session because a real problem had arisen. A man had been put down for one of the large churches of the conference. Some person had remarked that the man could not preach (which was not true). Bishop Martin let the members of the cabinet know how serious such statements were.[7]

AFTER FOUR YEARS

At the 1948 meeting of the South Central Jurisdiction in El Paso, Bishop Martin reported on his four years' work. He mentioned raising over $850,000 (on a quota of $732,000) for World Relief and Reconstruction, the establishing of 77 new churches, a 21 percent increase in church school enrollment, an increase of 45 percent in World Service and conference benevolences, an increase of 47 percent in the salaries of ministers, 40,223 additional church memberships by profession of faith and 55,711 by transfer, and other items.

But the gains were not simply in dollars and numbers. In evaluating the significance of the Martin years, Dr. Ewing T. Wayland, close friend and colaborer of the bishop as editor of the *Arkansas Methodist* and the *Louisiana Methodist*, later wrote: "Bishop and Mrs. Martin have through their leadership helped Methodists of this area to come to a new understanding of the greatness of the Christian Kingdom ideal. This perhaps is one of the most important achievements of these . . . years."[8]

Bishop Martin sought always to administer his conference sessions according to the *Discipline*—but to temper justice with mercy. One case in Arkansas involved a complicated interpretation of the *Discipline*'s intent regarding the length of time that could be allowed a pastor on the required course of study. The conference Board of Ministerial Training and Qualifications had located (that is, dropped from conference membership) one of the pastors for failing, as they understood the *Discipline*, to meet the requirement. Both the board and the bishop, however, had referred the matter for clarification to the Judicial Council. The Council ruled against the interpretation of the board and the bishop, but commended the spirit of both in these words: "Thus it appears that the Board of Ministerial Training . . . and Bishop Paul E. Martin . . . had shown Brother _____ great consideration and had dealt with him leniently and in a brotherly fashion."[9]

During the 1948-52 quadrennium expansion continued in the work of the area. Among achievements were such items as over $500,000 contributed to the Advance for Christ and His Church, new buildings at both Centenary College and Hendrix College, with large contributions from the T. L. James Co., Paul and Perry Brown, and Mr. W. A. Haynes (who gave over two million dollars for endowment to Centenary College), new buildings and more ministers for student work in Louisiana, new camp facilities, a new location in Little Rock for the Methodist Children's Home, a new maternity hospital in New Orleans for unwed mothers, the launching of the *Louisiana Methodist*, and more.[10]

His Style of Appointment-Making

Bishop Martin continued to seek ways to make appointments as effective as possible. Looking back on the 1946 Louisiana Conference appointments, he wrote one of the members[11] on June 21:

I was delighted . . . that the appointments turned out as they did, and I feel on the whole that it is a good list of appointments. I, too, was happy that it was possible to work Brother _____ into _____ Church in New Orleans. He will do a wonderful piece of work there. I think _____ will give excellent leadership to the _____ District. I feel also that _____ will be happier in the appointment in Alexandria.

Bishop Martin's philosophy in regard to several aspects of appointment-making is revealed in this letter to Dr. J. Henry Bowdon on May 21, 1948:

I can well understand why the members of your church would hate to give you up. You have done a fine piece of work there [Lake Charles], and of course they love Mrs. Bowdon and you. I have the feeling that you seem to have, that the same situations would result if you waited a time to make a change.

Of course, I do not want to make an unwise appointment, but it would seem that now is a good time for you to move. A district will likely not be open for a good while, and it would be particularly fortunate for you to be there at this period with your two children in school.

You can recognize that I am perfectly willing to take my responsibility in the matter, and yet you have been in the cabinet long enough to know that the attitude of a preacher has much to do with it. If a change is made, you must be willing to say to the people that you are agreeable to it. There is nothing that will hurt a church worse than for it to feel that the preacher wants to come back and that the bishop arbitrarily moves him. Certainly I would not want you to move unless you are perfectly willing to do so, but the people ought to know also. You are in the same situation that I was in when I left Greenville [Kavanaugh Church] to go to the Wichita Falls District.

On the same day the bishop wrote as follows to the Pastoral Relations Committee at the church:

I have considered Brother Bowdon for another appointment. The matter will not be finally decided until the Annual Conference session. If he is moved, it will only be because I feel that he is more needed in this other place. If such should be true, you can well understand I would give careful consideration to you and your church. In no sense does this mean that a change will come; but through the years of my administration, I have tried to be as sincere and frank with my people as I want them to be with me.

. . . I do have the responsibility of facing the whole program with many churches and districts involved, and sometimes I make changes because I feel that such should be done . . . whatever is done will be after careful and prayerful considerations. *

When Dr. Dana Dawson was elected bishop in July, 1948, Bishop Martin wrote one of the ministers regarding the new bishop's successor at First Church, Shreveport:

I appreciate your sentiments concerning a Louisiana man for First

Paul E. Martin astride a mule at the age of two, with his father, Dr. Charles E. Martin, at a health resort in Eureka Springs, Arkansas.

Paul E. Martin at the time of his graduation in 1915 from Paris (Texas) High School.

Dr. Paul E. Martin working at his desk in the study at First Methodist Church, Wichita Falls, Texas (1938-44).

Bishop Martin and Mrs. Joe J. Perkins of Wichita Falls, Texas—taken some years after he was pastor at the First Church there.

Bishops-elect Martin, left, and W. Angie Smith, just after their election in Tulsa, Oklahoma, in 1944.

Bishop and Mrs. Martin participate in the Centennial celebration of the
Louisiana Conference, at Opelousas on January 6, 1947.

Bishop and Mrs. Martin leaving on their trip to visit Methodist work in India in 1949.

Bishop and Mrs. Martin visit a baby fold (orphanage) in Bareilly, India, 1949.

Car purchased in 1947 by Methodists for missionary work in Czechoslovakia. Bishop Martin is second from left.

Bishop Martin conferring with Dr. Rajendra Prasad, President of India, on February 11, 1950.

Bishop Martin (second from left) at a reception in his honor at Hyderabad, India, in 1950. On his right is a Muslim high priest; on his left are a Parsee or Zoroastrian high priest and a Hindu high priest or sadhu.

Bishop and Mrs. Martin attending the General Conference of the Methodist Church in San Francisco, 1952.

Bishop Martin preaching at Oxford, England, 1951, during the Ecumenical Methodist Conference.

Bishop Martin (right) and Bishop Charles C. Selecman returning on the
S.S. *Media* from the Ecumenical Methodist Conference held in Oxford, England, 1951.

Bishop Martin (right), as chairman of the Editorial Division, Board of Education (1948-52), examines some of the work of Dr. C. A. Bowen, general secretary, and Mr. Morgan Stinemetz, art editor.

Bishop Martin (center) looks on as Dr. J. Philip Hyatt, one of the translators of the Revised Standard Version of the Bible, shows some pages from the new version. On the left is Dr. C. A. Bowen, editor of Church School Publications. (1952)

Bishop Martin (second from left) was vice president of the General Board of Education, 1948-56. On his right is Bishop Fred P. Carson, president of the Board; on his left are Bishop Paul N. Garber, vice president; Dr. John O. Gross, Dr. Henry M. Bullock, and Dr. John Q. Schisler, the three general secretaries of the Board in April, 1952.

Bishop Martin (right) presents a citation to Mr. J. J. Perkins at a meeting of the National Association of the Methodist Hospitals and Homes in Chicago, February 11, 1953.

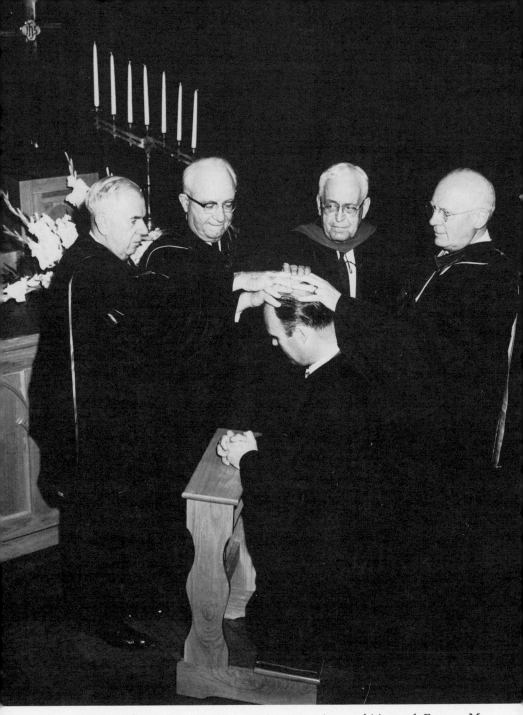

Bishop Martin, left, assists in the consecration as bishop of Eugene M. Frank (kneeling) on July 1, 1956; other bishops are A. Frank Smith, Ivan Lee Holt, and Edwin E. Voigt.

Bishop and Mrs. Martin (left) visiting with Bishop and Mrs. Arthur J. Moore en route to Singapore on board the S.S. *President Cleveland* in 1951.

Bishop Martin presides at the General Conference in Pittsburgh, Pennsylvania, on May 4, 1964.

Bishop Martin baptizing Wallace R. Shook, March 6, 1966.

Bishop Martin chats with two students at Kwansei Gakuin College, Nishinomiya, Japan, in 1965.

President Willis M. Tate of Southern Methodist University presents a plaque to Bishop and Mrs. Martin in recognition of the Bishop's leadership in the campaign for support of Texas Methodist colleges.

Governor John Connally of Texas chats with Bishop and Mrs. Martin at a dinner for the United Methodist Council of Bishops in Houston on April 21, 1965.

Bishop and Mrs. Martin at time of their retirement in 1968.

Church. I have demonstrated throughout the quadrennium the desire to give to the conferences all promotions [in appointments] possible. . . . This consideration must, however, be first in our mind: the appointment must be made on the basis of the man best suited for this tremendously important appointment. . . . We will give serious consideration to all men . . . [and] to the man best able to fill the place wherever he may come from.

"I have seen the Bishop so tired he could hardly go," comments the Rev. Jolly Harper, who served as a district superintendent, "yet continue to work into the night to try and work out a little happier appointment for some unhappy brother or church."

Obviously not every appointment could be completely satisfactory to all parties concerned, but there is one interesting story about an appointment that was heartily commended by a non-Methodist. When the North Arkansas Conference met in Walnut Ridge in 1945 Bishop Martin received a letter that read: "Dear Sir, I'm called an infidel because I do not believe the Bible. Am also called an atheist, and a naturalist. But I would hate like H—— to live in a town without a 'preacher' like Bro. Prewitt. Won't you please send him back."

As soon as the appointments were made, the letter-writer called and asked, "Did you send Brother Prewitt back?" When the Bishop answered "Yes," the caller responded, "Thank God."[12]

CONTINUED PROGRESS

During the third and fourth quadrennia in which Bishop Martin served Arkansas and Louisiana institutional progress continued. Ministers' salaries increased, church membership gained, new churches were established, and new buildings were erected. The two colleges added more new buildings and endowment. Mr. and Mrs. J. M. Willson of Floydada, Texas, endowed a lectureship at each college, and Wesley Foundation work expanded, with new buildings and new personnel made available. Camping facilities were enlarged, and a new hospital was acquired in Monroe, Louisiana.

Noteworthy were three special endowments: Hendrix College increased its endowment by more than a half-million; Robert J. Bynum of New Orleans joined Rayne Memorial Church after he was seventy years old and left three quarters of a million dollars to Centenary College; and the Louisiana Methodist Home at Ruston gained about a half-million dollars in endowment.[13]

But not only were these church institutions better financed—they were, more importantly, more closely related to the church. Laymen became more acutely aware of these various channels through which the church could witness to and serve the world. And they were increasingly gaining a wider vision of the meaning of Christian commitment in personal life and in social relationships.

One significant and far-reaching proposal that Bishop Martin made to the Arkansas conferences was that they merge into one body. The issue was debated vigorously and approved by the North Arkansas Conference, but rejected by the Little Rock Conference. A dozen years after he left, this issue was still being considered—with Little Rock now favoring it but North Arkansas against.

A DIFFICULT, UNHAPPY PERIOD

The last quadrennium, however, brought to the bishop the most difficult and unhappy period in his ministry—the time of the integration of the Little Rock schools. He has written about it in some detail in his "Reflections." It was a difficult and unhappy time because there was no way to avoid conflict and a certain amount of open controversy. And Bishop Martin was not temperamentally congenial to this way of gaining one's objective, as we have clearly seen by his whole life-style across the years.

The Martins were on an overseas assignment when the trouble began, and by the time they returned, emotions were stirred and many persons embittered. Bishop W. Kenneth Pope, who was Bishop Martin's successor in 1960, states that some Methodist laymen were simply swept off their feet in the tide of frenzied hate that developed. Most of the ministers held firm for obeying the law—or at least for using legal channels for opposition to the situation. Aubrey G. Walton and J. Kenneth Shamblin were among the pastors of larger churches who allied themselves with the bishop in appealing for reason, justice, and brotherhood.[14] E. D. Galloway, the District Superintendent in Little Rock, was a source of strength and power to the bishop, and gave significant leadership to the churches during this conflict.

Most of those who opposed Bishop Martin's stand for lawful actions and for a relationship to one's fellow man of love rather than hate were either anonymous harassers or non-Methodists; but there was some open Methodist dissent.

Bishop Martin said on a telecast on October 26, 1958, that his effort was to serve as "a minister of reconciliation"; he deplored the fact that nearly four thousand boys and girls in Little Rock were at that time being deprived of the opportunity to attend public school.[15]

In a sermon at First Church, Little Rock, he called on Methodists "to avoid the world's evil tempers; its hatreds, its prejudices, and its pride." Dr. E. Clifton Rule looks back on that period for the bishop as "a trial by fire," and says it "was a difficult road." Another minister wrote him: "You have been called to serve during a dark time in our state. But . . . the Methodist Church has come through, it has not silenced its voice. . . ." Another person wrote: "I am glad that we have a Methodist bishop in Arkansas who is guided by God's will and who follows an enlightened conscience."[16]

In such a situation it was inevitable that some would feel that he acted "too little and too late," and that others would feel that he acted "too much and too fast." Fortunately, those closest to him, and on whom he depended most for assurance and support, gave him that undergirding. Dr. and Mrs. C. M. Reeves wrote of their concern, pointing out, "In His kingdom, bleeding and blessing go hand in hand; pain and progress are inseparable."[17]

A good summing up of this experience comes from Bishop Walton:

Though he had many rough experiences and endured harassment, as did many others, he steadfastly retained his kind and compassionate attitude toward all and witnessed daily for the faith that was his. He laid a good foundation in human relations in both states, which made it possible for those of us who followed to build upon. Though the last four years of Bishop Martin in Arkansas and Louisiana were, without doubt, the most difficult of his stay in this area, I have always felt that they were perhaps his best and most constructive years.[18]

LIGHTER MOMENTS

During the Little Rock residence there were also moments of humor for the Martins. Bishop Aubrey G. Walton tells of the time when Pratt Remmel, a member of First Church, Little Rock, was elected mayor of the city:

He was very fond of Bishop Martin. One morning he called the Bishop on the telephone and asked if he would attend the inauguration services for the new mayor and offer a prayer on that occasion. Bishop Martin thanked him for the invitation and said he regretted that he would be out of the city at that time. Mr. Remmel was very sorry that he was not to be available, but requested the Bishop to keep the new mayor in his prayers. Then im-

pulsively he asked, "Why don't you offer a prayer for me right now?" The
Bishop replied that he was not accustomed to prayer over the telephone but
that he saw no reason not to do so. As he was right in the middle of his
prayer, Mrs. Martin entered the room. She was puzzled: she knew her husband was a devout man, but did he actually have a telephone line to God?[19]

The bishop naturally received all types of introductions as he went
from place to place. He chuckles as he tells of one in New Orleans, when
the pastor was probably inspired by the choir's singing "A Tree Planted
by the River." The pastor compared the church to a tree, saying that the
fundamental beliefs are the roots, the lay members are the trunk or body,
and the ministers are symbolized by birds on the various branches. Wax-
ing eloquent, he continued, "On the top branches in all their glorious
plumage are the bishops." He paused and smiled as he said, "We have
the bird with us today!" When the bishop arose, he replied, "That is correct. I am a Martin."

WEARING TIMES

It is obvious that these were wearing years for Bishop Martin, especially in the 1956-60 quadrennium. At all times he maintained a heavy
work schedule. As early as the fall of 1945 one of his longtime friends
urged him to "take it a bit easier." The Bishop in replying wrote: "I
realize that I have been under a pretty heavy schedule, but I have been
so anxious to give the leadership that I felt I should that I have just kept
on going."

On March 24, 1950, the Bishop wrote again: "I am glad we can have
the meeting at Alexandria on April 11. . . . This is the only period in
which I have any free time until May." And on July 11, 1952, he wrote:
"I know that I cannot continue at the heavy pace I have been going, but
you know something of the demands upon a person today and of my
great interest in all the work of the Church."

On December 1, 1953, Bishop Martin wrote: "I have had about the
heaviest schedule I have ever known since my return home." And on the
next May 21 he wrote: "I am afraid I will not be able to get any rest
before Conference, but I am going to try this summer to carry a lighter
program."

In March, 1958, he had a fairly serious health warning, with a heart
involvement, and was in the hospital in Monroe, Louisiana for twelve
days, unknown to almost everyone. Dr. Ewing T. Wayland, editor of
the two state papers, learned of the illness and drove at once from Little

Rock to the hospital. Mrs. Martin let him see the bishop, and the first thing he said to Ewing was, "Ewing, you and I both just have to begin to take things easier." "Even in his initial heart attack," comments Dr. Wayland, "he was thinking not of his own troubles but of the well-being of others. He recovered from that attack and in due time was again spending himself with about the same speed as before."[20]

MANY RICH EXPERIENCES

As a whole, the years in Arkansas and Louisiana brought many rich experiences to Bishop and Mrs. Martin and to the people with whom they were associated. Among those not already mentioned were the overseas trips to the mission fields and to ecumenical gatherings, on some of which the area raised money to send Mrs. Martin also. Bishop Martin has told about these in his "Reflections." There were at least three series of lectures given in the area (and others outside)—the Jones Memorial Lectures at Rayne Memorial Church, New Orleans, in February, 1951; the Raney Lectures at Pulaski Heights Church, Little Rock, in March, 1952; and the Goddard Memorial Lectures at Goddard Memorial Church, Fort Smith, in February, 1957.

Among the many honors awarded the bishop during this period was the conferring of the 33rd degree in Scottish Rite Masonry in 1957. Mr. Joshua K. Shepherd was largely responsible for this high honor being awarded to Bishop Martin.

Bishop Martin served as chairman of the trustees for Mt. Sequoyah Assembly at Fayetteville, a jurisdictional enterprise, and guided it in needed expansion and improvement. One of the new buildings erected there in 1957 was a chapel, given by their loyal friends, Mr. and Mrs. J. J. Perkins, and named in honor of Paul and Mildred Martin. Another part of this building was a gift of the T. L. James family of Ruston, also bound by close ties to the Martins.

The contributions Mrs. Martin made to the work in the area were appropriately recognized when Hendrix College conferred on her the honorary degree of Doctor of Laws on May 3, 1959. (Incidentally, at the same time she was president of the Wives of the Council of Bishops.) The citation from the college pointed out that "though lacking the title and serving without portfolio, [she had] been for fifteen years the highly regarded and deeply appreciated assistant bishop of the Arkansas-Louisiana Area."[21]

The General Conference in 1960 established a twelve-year limit on episcopal service to an area, though it was not retroactive. Until this action was taken many members of the area were hoping—even expecting —that Bishop Martin would be returned. Back in 1955 Dr. J. Q. Schisler, a ministerial member of the area and a wise and respected General Board educator, wrote the bishop that ministers and laymen in the area wanted him "to remain their bishop to the time of [his] retirement." Again shortly before the Jurisdictional Conference in 1960 he wrote again: "The boys [meaning the preachers—and laymen] seemed to be afraid they were going to lose you. It would warm your heart to know what they say about your years of service in that area."[22]

Nevertheless, a move seemed the wise thing. It would be in the spirit of the new twelve-year tenure, which he had already exceeded. He had only eight more years as active bishop, and if he waited four years that would leave only four years on a new area—too short a time to become well acquainted and to carry out the kind of program he would wish to do. And the difficult times over integration had left scars—emotional and physical. A new start elsewhere held the promise of another bright chapter in his life and ministry.

CHAPTER NINE

Serving the Houston Area

IN 1960 the South Central Jurisdictional Conference assigned Bishop Martin to give episcopal supervision to the Houston Area. The area included the Texas Conference and the Rio Grande Conference. Both conferences—and the area as a whole—had several unique characteristics.

The Houston Area was and is the strongest area in Texas, and among the dozen strongest areas in the denomination. In 1960 the area had over 220,000 members and 644 ministers, and the membership had contributed over $14,000,000 for all causes. There were 564 pastoral charges, and property was valued at nearly $85,000,000. There were many strong churches in the area, and during the Martin era First Church, Houston, regained its earlier status of having the largest membership in the connection.

The Texas Conference holds the original name of the first conference in Texas, organized in 1840 while Texas was still a republic. The conference takes great pride in its historicity. In 1960, before Bishop Martin was assigned as its bishop, it had issued a volume of historical data under the title, *Texas Conference Methodism on the March*, edited by one of its members, the Rev. C. A. West.

Another unique feature of the area at that time was the inclusion of the only remaining conference based on a language difference—the Rio Grande. This conference also has a long and significant history, now being written (at the encouragement of Bishop Martin, Dean Joseph D. Quillian, and others) by Dr. Alfredo Nanez of the Perkins School of Theology. Its boundaries overlap a half-dozen other conferences.

A Different Texas from the 1930s

When Bishop Martin returned to the Lone Star State he found a different Texas from the one he had known in the 1930s. In 1934, 40 percent of the state's population was on the farm; in 1960 it was only slightly over 7 percent.[1] Another 18 percent were rural nonfarm, leaving 75 percent as urban. This shift had brought significant changes to the state—and nowhere more than in Houston, the state's largest city, with a million and a quarter residents and the nation's third largest seaport. This shift in population brought problems to both rural and urban areas. Bishop Martin himself later described these issues in this way: "The constant shift of population from rural area, young people seeking jobs, pockets where racial tensions develop, poverty stricken areas, demand flexible forms and new patterns of service."

The nerve center of the conference was Houston, by 1960 developing into one of the great cities of the South. George Fuermann described the city in 1957 in his *Reluctant Empire: The Mind of Texas*:

Largest city in Texas, largest in the South if Baltimore is not South, largest in America with racial segregation, Houston sprawls on the Gulf plain, coaxing the future. Oil producer, oil refiner, oil bookkeeper, gas sender to the nation, deep-water port fifty miles inland, anthill of large law firms, it takes traditions from the present. . . . Church town, medical center, university city; air conditioned, stewing in education conflicts, breathing assurance. . . . One of every eight Texans lives in Metropolitan Houston. . . .
. . . The people's character is illumined by a Main Street sign on the First Baptist Church. Near the center of the business district, the sign spells "Jesus Saves" in electric lights. Contradicting the evangelist Billy Graham, religion pervades the city's life.[2]

Place for a New Bishop

Such was the area into which the new bishop set forth to help make the religion of Jesus Christ real to persons and influential in all of their relations. As he took up this task he did so with a sense of assurance and anticipation. Under his leadership the Arkansas-Louisiana Area had made significant progress. His first episcopal assignment had been well handled in spite of difficult issues at times. Recognition had also come to him for the excellent Episcopal Message he had delivered in San Antonio at the 1960 Jurisdictional Conference. It was one of the better Episcopal Messages in the annals of the Jurisdiction.

The new bishop was following one of the most influential Methodists Houston has ever known—Bishop A. Frank Smith. Smith had gone there in 1922 as pastor of First Methodist Church, and after election as bishop in 1930 had kept his home there as he served various episcopal areas. Thus he had been a prominent figure in Houston circles for nearly forty years, and many of his friends were not certain that they could transfer their loyalty and affection to a "new" leader.

Fortunately, Bishop Smith had encouraged the assignment of Bishop Martin to Houston, and this opened many doors for the younger man. Even so, it was difficult for some to use the new name for the bishop. In fact, one embarrassed Methodist had a slip of the tongue in introducing Bishop Martin at a meeting at St. Luke's Church soon after the change, and presented him as "Bishop Smith." Bishop Martin's graciousness and sense of humor soon had the red-faced man at ease.[3]

The new leader undertook his supervision of the area with enthusiasm and care. He studied carefully the problems and opportunities of the area. He followed his previous practice of getting to know every preacher and his family personally and demonstrating his belief that "Everybody Is Somebody."

RIO GRANDE CONFERENCE

He soon came to the conclusion that the Rio Grande Conference was functioning more on the basis of a mission than a conference. He encouraged the conference to rethink its structure, including the conference board organization. The conference made some changes in board membership, and began to function more truly as an annual conference.

Bishop Martin worked in other ways also in strengthening the work of the Rio Grande Conference. He assisted in opening one new district, and encouraged his coworkers as they erected twenty-nine church buildings, five new educational buildings, and twenty-five new parsonages in 1960-64. Seven new congregations were organized and three new preaching places established during the same time. An endowment fund was established to provide more adequate pensions for the Rio Grande pastors. He assisted in efforts that resulted in the erection of a new physical education building and a new president's home at Lydia Patterson Institute. When a new director was needed for the Institute, he helped choose one of the most experienced and influential persons available—the Rev. Alfredo Nanez. Looking back on this aspect of work, he says that if he had it to do again he would learn Spanish, rather than to have to work through an interpreter.

Dr. Alfredo Nanez comments that Bishop Martin had appealed to the Mexican Americans of the Rio Grande Conference because he changed their Latin concept of the office of bishop. They had a concept of authority, aloofness, and power, whereas Bishop Martin had filled the role of a chief pastor, human, and even gentle. But, he continued, "make no mistake, this gentleness has not been a sign of weakness, for many a time in the cabinet or on the floor of the conference, like last year [1967], we have seen . . . his indignation for sloppiness and work poorly done." [4]

THE TEXAS CONFERENCE UNREST

It soon became clear to Bishop Martin that, as one conference member put it, "an upheaval had started in conference leadership" before he arrived.[5] This was revealed most obviously in a radical shift in the election of delegates to the General and Jurisdictional Conferences of 1956 and 1960. Of course, there is normally some shifting of delegates from quadrennium to quadrennium, but there was more involved this time.

The leader of the 1956 delegation of ministers was not elected to the 1960 General Conference, but was the sixth delegate to the Jurisdictional Conference. Three others who had been delegates since 1948 were not elected to either conference. Likewise, only three lay delegates out of seven from the 1956 delegation were elected in 1960 to General Conference.

This shifting of delegates was generally due to the influence of a group of young ministers, some of whom organized later as Ministers for Church Renewal. When Bishop Martin arrived he found this shift in leadership under way. Members of the Renewal group felt that he evidently saw this as an opportunity to start afresh, and as one of them put it, "he made a very honest (and usually successful) attempt to spread the base of participation and power, and to open up the appointive process to full cabinet influence."[6] As district superintendents reached the end of their terms, they were replaced by younger men.

In Bishop Martin's second quadrennium the younger ministers organized as Ministers for Church Renewal, and later changed the name to

United Methodists for Church Renewal. This movement was similar to others across the nation in various denominations. Dr. Albert C. Outler of Perkins School of Theology called this situation across the church the result of a "vivid despair and disenchantment" on the part of many ministers. In November, 1967, he called for basic reform in policy to help ease the situation. He deplored the

> tragic deadlock between those who believe they could make the system work better if they were in charge, and those who realize (quite rightly, too) that our present leadership is doing as effective a job as can be expected or demanded of flesh and blood, *within the system* as it now stands. Too many of our self-styled reformers strike me as destructively hostile in their opposition to the *status quo....* I have come to believe that nothing short of basic constitutional change will suffice for the reform and renewal of The United Methodist Church that most of us profess to desire.[7]

In spite of differences of opinion on various issues, some leaders of the renewal group maintained openness toward "the establishment," revealed in this letter one of them wrote Bishop Martin in 1967:[8]

DEAR BISHOP MARTIN:

Those of us who talked with you last Monday came away with a new picture of our Bishop. We saw an openness and concern that we had not seen before, and were helped and encouraged by it.

Thank you for taking the time. We needed to talk with you. Our own commitment to the Church will be influenced over the years by what happened in those minutes we spent with you.

These are exciting days for us all.

Sincerely,

In the later years of Bishop Martin's tenure at Houston the situation became more acute. In the opinion of one commentator some of the younger men felt that they were not being advanced as fast as they should, and that the district superintendents were not recognizing them adequately or giving the conference the leadership it needed. Therefore, as the conference of 1967 approached, some of them organized a concentrated campaign to elect "new leadership," with at least a part of them being the "old leaders" of the 1950s.[9]

Many of those involved in the Renewal group were a part of this attempt to select a slate of delegates, so that in the eyes of many in the conference this political group and the Renewal group were one and the same. This was not true, however, as many were in the Renewal group who did not participate in the political push, and vice versa.

Some may have thought of this political group as providing a direct attack upon Bishop Martin's administration. However, it was more an attempt to lay the base for a change in leadership in the conference with the upcoming change of bishops.

"MOVING TOGETHER"

In 1967-68 the bishop and other leaders in the conference planned and launched a program called "Moving Together in Christian Faith, Obedience, and Action," which was obviously an effort to deal with some of the concerns of the Renewal group. The program as outlined covered eight areas: renewal, recruitment, leadership development, lay ministry, Christian unity, missions support, Christian action, and membership growth. The literature recommended readings in the works of such writers as Colin Williams, Martin E. Marty, Robert Raines, George W. Webber, Dietrich Bonhoeffer, Howard Grimes, Hendrik Kraemer, Albert C. Outler, Harold Fey, and Harold Bosley.

However, the Renewal group was not happy with the program proposed. An editorial appeared in their *A Journal of Opinion* saying the program "has been virtually ignored by most of the ministers,... it has no effect on our life together... and [is] of no real consequence whatsoever."[10]

When the conference met in June, 1967, Bishop Martin preached on the program, giving a rationale for it and making these observations:

We justify our failures by saying what a contribution we could make to the world if we...had someone else's opportunities.... How varied are the places we serve.... Wherever we labor, it is a part of God's work, and the people we serve are His children.

This is no time to emphasize our differences. It is a time to proclaim the fact that we are all followers of Christ.

Then in a fairly direct reference to the "generation gap" he quoted from Henry Barnett:

> Old men have wisdom to give to the young,
> And young men have words for the old;
>
> . . . .
>
> For wisdom lies not in Age or in Youth
> Each has, and each shares, and each learns.[11]

One further development is reported by a member of the conference:

The Renewal group continued until the annual conference session of June, 1968. It seemed to many of us that their [feelings] . . . reached a climax at conference (Bishop Martin's last) . . . Bishop Martin remained as calm and as patient as humanly possible. . . . They wanted certain assignments made. . . . Bishop Martin and the cabinet gave them appointments and promotions exactly the same as we would have if they had not been members of the group.[12]

During these eight years much of what has just been described involved a relatively small percent of the conference membership, and much of it occurred behind the scenes. As a whole, the years in Houston can be described as always challenging, sometimes exciting, mostly happy, occasionally difficult, and frequently fruitful.

They even had their humorous incidents as well, of course. Bishop Martin relates one of these:

During annual conference sessions we usually stayed at the Lamar Hotel, near First Church. One night just before dinner a young minister's wife excitedly knocked on our door. She had almost panicked. Her dress was far too small, and the zipper was stuck and would not close. My wife called me to help, and I responded by squeezing while she pulled. I suppose that was the most undignified episcopal act on record, but it was highly appreciated!

A Multitude of Achievements

There were many achievements during these years. One was the bishop's effort to deepen the Christian commitment of preachers and laity in the conference. One of the ways he went about this was his use of the column in the conference edition of the *Texas Methodist* called "Our Bishop Speaks." Instead of using it to promote causes and projects, he dealt with matters of faith and belief. Typical titles he used were: "Life and Death," "The Real Christmas," "Easter Message," "Thanksgiving Message," "What Do You Know for Sure?" "There's 'Ope Ahead," "The Lord Will Know," and "All Men Are Brothers."

Another example of his efforts at lifting spiritual horizons was in his use of hymns during annual conference sessions. He used a combination of old favorites and excellent new hymns (new to many of the singers, that is). A few examples are illustrative: "And Are We Yet Alive," "Blessed Assurance," "Rise Up, O Men of God," "Guide Me, O Thou

Great Jehovah," "Christ Whose Glory Fills the Skies," "Amazing Grace," "God of Grace and God of Glory," and "When Morning Gilds the Skies."

Bishop Martin's years in Houston were marked by numerous ecumenical activities. In 1963 he gave the graduating address at the Baylor University Medical College, using one of his favorite emphases, "Everybody Is Somebody." He had numerous requests for copies of the address. He was commended by Dean Stanley Wolson of the Baptist institution for stressing that "when a doctor exercises his skill, he is treating a person, not a disease." During the times when Cuban refugees were arriving at the Houston airport he joined other religious leaders in a ceremony greeting them in person. In September, 1964, he participated in the consecration of the new Episcopal bishop, the Rev. Scott Field Bailey, in Christ Church Cathedral. Other participants included Roman Catholics and Greek Orthodox representatives.[13]

At the 1964 session of the Texas Conference visiting speakers included Bishop John L. Morkovsky, a Catholic; Rabbi Hyman Judah Schachtel; and Dr. Karl M. Parker, director of the Houston Association of Churches. He established close personal relationships with these and other persons of various faiths.

Specific cooperative ecumenical projects were carried out, such as the shipping of wheat to India. In May, 1966, he spoke at a ceremony when 21,000 tons of the grain were being loaded in Houston, a combined project of Church World Service (a National Council of Churches agency) and Catholic Relief Service. He was the speaker at a Reformation Day observance at the Music Hall in Houston on October 29, 1961, sponsored by the Association of Churches.

Many calls were made on Bishop Martin for what was essentially pastoral care. These included such services as conducting or assisting in funerals of a number of persons, including former governor William P. Hobby, Bishop A. Frank Smith, Mrs. A. Frank Smith, and several ministers of the conference. One man once said to Dr. W. Harrison Baker, longtime friend of the bishop, "It would be easier to die if Paul Martin was near." Other such pastoral services were Sunday worship events, preaching missions, revivals, and special sermons at countless churches; many cornerstone layings, church dedications, baptisms, and weddings; radio and television appearances; and dinners given each year to the students attending Perkins and their wives from the Texas Conference during Ministers' Week.

INTEGRATION OF CONFERENCES

This era under Bishop Martin's leadership was the time when the delicate decision regarding the union of the Negro Texas Conference and the white Texas Conference was accomplished. This union was made easier through the close working relationship developed by Bishop Martin and Bishop Noah W. Moore, Jr., who was in charge of the Central Jurisdiction's Southwestern Area. In 1964 Bishop Moore moved from New Orleans to Houston, and the two bishops worked very closely together in the preparation of the merger of the two conferences. When the Moores reached Houston the Martins called on them and presented a beautifully bound book on the history of Texas. In April, 1965, when the Council of Bishops met in Houston, Bishops Martin and Moore were joint hosts to the gathering.

During the 1964-68 quadrennium a climate was developed that made it possible in June, 1967, for the Texas Conference to approve union of the two conferences by a vote of 506 to 16. Actual merger occurred in 1969.

INSTITUTIONAL ADVANCE

Bishop Martin committed himself to help undergird the various institutions of the area. He did this both publicly and privately. He sent a check for use at one of the conference institutions, and in reply received a letter saying, "This is the first time in a quarter of a century that we have received a check from a Methodist bishop." He participated in public rallies to raise funds for various causes.[14]

In March, 1965, he dedicated five major buildings at Lon Morris College, Jacksonville, most of them built from gifts that Bishop Martin had encouraged, at least indirectly, by his loyalty to the church's work in education. The buildings include the R. W. Fair Hall, the E. G. C. Scurlock Cafeteria–Student Center, the Paul W. Pewitt Science Hall, the Simon and Louise Henderson Library, and the Jimmie Owen Administration Building. In dedicating these buildings the bishop stressed the vital place of the church and the church college in the cause of freedom and progress.

During his tenure the conference acquired a new hospital in Baytown, three homes for the elderly (Moody House in Galveston, Happy Harbor in LaPorte, and Crestview in Bryan), and a new Vivian and R. E. Smith Headquarters Building in Houston, a three-story building that will serve the conference for many years. A nine-million-dollar addition was made to the Methodist Hospital in Houston in 1963, which he helped dedicate, and in the course of the next quadrennium a ten-million-dollar Fondren and Brown Orthopedic and Cardio-Vascular Research Center was almost finished.

The consecration service and formal opening of the Vivian and R. E. (Bob) Smith Methodist Building in Houston was held on October 20, 1967. This handsome and useful conference headquarters is located on Houston's Main Street, and houses the offices of the bishop, the district superintendents, and the conference staff. It also has a chapel, a prayer room, a conference room, and a cabinet room. Mr. and Mrs. Smith made the building possible through an outstanding gift. The property will serve the conference for generations to come.

Church leaders present at the consecration service included the Most Reverend John Morkovsky, Apostolic Administrator of the Roman Catholic Diocese of Galveston-Houston; the Right Reverend J. Milton Richardson of the Episcopal Diocese of Texas; Dr. Hyman Judah Schachtel, Chief Rabbi of Congregation Beth Israel; and the Reverend Robert E. Hayes, Houston District Superintendent of the Central Jurisdiction of The Methodist Church. Mayor Louie Welch also attended the service, representing laymen of the city. In honor of Bishop and Mrs. Martin a striking plaque and portraits of the two have been placed in the building.

Dr. Charles L. Allen, pastor of First Church, Houston, has written that had it not been for Bishop Martin's vision, energy, and dedication, the conference would not now have this building. "Had he not acted when he did I believe the beautiful location we now have would have been forever beyond our grasp. A lesser man than he would not have been willing to enter into that large an undertaking so close to the time of retirement. This beautiful and useful building will long serve to remind us of his leadership."[15]

Bishop Martin encouraged the progress of the Methodist Hospital in Houston achieved under the leadership of its administrator, Mr. Ted Bowen and his capable staff. Mr. Bowen inspired confidence in individuals to give vast sums of money for the expansion of the facilities of the institution. Mrs. W. W. Fondren is one of the great philanthropists and a most capable and helpful member of the Methodist Hospital's board of trustees.

Is was in connection with his relationship to Mr. Bowen that the bishop developed a close relationship with many of the Houston doctors.

Dr. Hatch Cummings was the personal physician for the Martins, and Dr. Ray Goens not only was an able physician but gave constant support in the conference program. He was a delegate to general and jurisdictional conferences several times. Dr. Michael DeBakey won the admiration of the bishop for his well-known skill as a heart surgeon, and also for the quality of his life. When Bishop Martin suffered a critical heart attack in Ruston, Louisiana, Dr. DeBakey telephoned Mildred offering to charter a plane to come to see him. The friendship has continued to the present day, and a feeling of mutual admiration exists between the two men.

Through the generosity of Mr. Bowen special equipment for brain surgery was provided for Dr. Ding Wik Kiu of Hong Kong, whom the bishop had earlier visited in Hong Kong. When the Duke of Windsor came to Houston for heart surgery, Mr. Bowen and Dr. DeBakey requested Bishop Martin to serve as chaplain to the Windsors.

Bishop Martin's great interest in the space program is reflected in his comment:

One of the most exciting events to take place during the years in Houston was the development of the N.A.S.A. program. The so-called fantastic idea of a man walking on the moon became an accepted reality. The space center located near the city brought brilliant and adventurous scientists who were dedicated church members. Many of them belonged to our church. Thomas Stafford carried with him one of my Bibles as he journeyed into space. I proudly point in my study to an autographed picture given by him after a thrilling flight of two great crafts joined in space.

STATEWIDE OBLIGATIONS

The bishop of the Houston area also had certain statewide Methodist obligations. He served on numerous Methodist state boards. One was the Texas Methodist Planning Commission, where he made a major presentation in February, 1964. He made the major address on April 2, 1965, in recognition of the establishment of an $80,000 collection of books for the library at the Institute of Religion in Houston, made possible by gifts in honor of the eightieth birthday of Mr. J. S. Bridwell of Wichita Falls. He made the address at the dedication of SMU's Science Information Center in November, 1961, and helped dedicate the new Wesley Foundation Building at A&M College in November, 1963. He helped inaugurate Dr. L. Durwood Fleming as president of Southwestern University in 1961. Fleming had joined the North Texas Conference while Dr.

Martin was pastor at Wichita Falls, and was elected to head the university from the pastorate of St. Luke's Church in Houston. The bishop assisted in dedicating the Zimmerman Home and the W. W. Fondren Home on the Waco Methodist Home campus, and officiated at the dedication of the new Methodist Mission Home in San Antonio. He was the preacher at the Texas Pastors School at Southwestern University in July, 1963.

During these years Bishop Martin was quietly the key person in solving some delicate and difficult situations. Concerning one of these situations a prominent younger leader in the church wrote the following to Bishop Martin:

> I had some strong convictions about what I considered to be right in the situation and you were not aware of it; but I was aware of you and how you were handling the situation. I knew in my own mind that the circumstances . . . could be resolved if you stood firm and maintained your integrity. . . . I shall always be grateful [that] when the chips were down, you turned out to be the kind of person I had thought you to be.... If you had yielded under the pressure and compromised some of the convictions which I held, I am not sure what the course of my ministry or life would have been from that point on.[16]

The bishop's goal of good appointment-making continued. Not all appointments could be perfect, but they could be as good as careful study, humane considerations, and prayerful guidance could provide. Several conference members expressed their approval of some of them: "I have heard surprise and delight on your appointment of the last three district superintendents," and "I'm one of the many who appreciate all you have done . . . to heal the divisions. . . . I think this healing work was shown, among many things, by your appointment of _____," and "Thank you . . . for your insistence of 'no politics' in appointment-making."[17]

Many Demands

The Houston years were the last ones before retirement, and they brought many demands. The pace of Bishop and Mrs. Martin can be seen from this letter she wrote to her good friend, Mrs. J. J. Perkins, in March, 1966, from Texas Wesleyan College, Fort Worth, where the bishop was giving the Willson Lectures on the overall theme of "Man's Search for Meaning":

We are *busy*.... We are in our third week of being away from home except for weekends when Paul has had three services each Sunday and working Saturdays on his messages and mail. Next week in Galveston we have the Jurisdictional Convocation. All of the boards will meet and we will have speakers.... Paul and I will get home Friday night and go to Galveston Monday.

Then the following week we will go to our meeting of the Conference W.S.C.S. and Paul will hold a cabinet meeting while there with the District Superintendents.

We will have appts. in the district with Neal [Cannon] and Fae before getting home.[18]

One of the demands on his time, energy, and thought was also a happy privilege—and honor. It was an invitation to deliver the Fondren Lectures at Southern Methodist University in February, 1968. These lectures, begun in 1920, had included some of the great names in American Protestantism, such as Robert E. Speer, Sherwood Eddy, James Moffatt, Frances J. McConnell, Charles R. Brown, Edwin Lewis, Reinhold Niebuhr, John C. Bennett, Ralph W. Sockman, Langdon Gilkey, Nels Ferre, W. E. Sangster, Edgar Brightman, and John Deschner.

Bishop Martin's series was entitled Qualities of Greatness, and it met with warm, even glowing, responses from many persons. Among these were Dean Joseph D. Quillian, President Willis M. Tate, Bishop Aubrey G. Walton, and others. Perhaps one of the most unique descriptions of the lectures was this one by Dr. Alfred Knox, editor of the *Arkansas Methodist* and the *Louisiana Methodist:*

It was common talk around the campus of Southern Methodist University last week that "somebody goofed." For the first time in the memory of modern man all three lecturers for Ministers' Week had something to say, could say it distinctly, and used a vocabulary that even the most simple of us could understand. It was the consensus that the committee would never let it happen again! It simply isn't academic—whatever that is.

Bishop Paul E. Martin was the star as the Fondren Lecturer—singing his "swan song" prior to his retirement next summer. His emphasis was on the need for Christians to regain their confidence and faith in God's power. He said, "I am convinced that in this period of uncertainty we need to see the contributions that Christian faith can make to the world."

Warning that one of the greatest dangers to a vital faith is a wrong concept of God, he pointed out that God must not be regarded as an errand boy. He said "It is discouraging to find so many young people who should be adventurous, but who are characterized by lack of concern and responsibility. . . ." The visitors to Ministers' Week went away talking to themselves —but they knew what they were saying.

On Balance

As Bishop Martin closed his tenure of the Houston Area one could see fine achievements in certain phases of the work, other aspects still unfinished, and some still neglected by the churches. Financially, the record showed the growing affluence of Methodists—and the generosity of some of them. World Service giving had increased from $509,874 in 1960 to $911,381 in 1968; total giving from $14,161,437 to $17,660,-036. The value of church properties had gone from $84,759,326 to $121,248,219.

There were 682 ministers in 1968, thirty-eight more than eight years earlier; of this increase twenty ministers were in the Rio Grande Conference. Membership had increased by over 30,000, though there were fewer pastoral charges.

There were many signs of deepened commitment on the part of ministers and laity. Many of them testify that the Martins "inspired us all to be our best."

A prominent judge wrote, "You are a great source of encouragement to me," and a banker said, "You make one exceptionally proud to be a Methodist."[19] But there were others who were still lukewarm in commitment, desultory in attendance, and grudging in giving. Some were unhappy, others puzzled, and still others angered at some of the ways the church was trying to meet the needs of the poor. And Houston and East Texas (and the world, for that matter) still had not settled the issues between black and white, brown and white, rich and poor, outcast and privileged, sinful man and righteous God.

Bishop Martin had said in San Antonio in 1960 in the Jurisdictional Episcopal Message: "We have witnessed the ugly flowering of bitterness and bigotry.... Barriers of bitterness have been erected even between persons of the same race." Those flowers were still blooming in some yards. But he had also issued a high challenge to South Central Methodists: "When time has passed and ugly passions have died and reason is restored, let it be said that the church did not fail in one of its greatest opportunities."

His closing paragraphs in the 1960 Episcopal Message typify the message he had been preaching for forty-six years:

Actually spiritual hunger is revealed in the frustrating sense of emptiness and dissatisfaction which characterize many people. Their fears cry out for the deliverance that is brought only by a profound religious faith.

If the Church can declare the major emphases which have always made it great; if it boldly moves out in new paths; if it will assume its proper leadership against all un-Christian conditions; if it will proclaim a faith of world character and importance, an unsurpassed opportunity for accomplishing the salvation of mankind awaits it.[20]

CHAPTER TEN

Serving the Church at Large

EVERY METHODIST BISHOP must serve on numerous general boards and agencies of the church, along with other ministers and lay persons. The best minds and hearts of the church are needed to help plan, guide, and supervise the churchwide enterprises of mission, evangelism, education, benevolence, and social concerns.

Strong leadership is needed from across the church in order to make sure that the general agencies truly follow the will of the church, and not their own plans. At the same time, representatives of the church at large have only a limited amount of time to give to agency policies and plans, and much of the work must be left to the agency staff.

Bishop Paul E. Martin was called on frequently to assist in the leadership of general agencies, and his role in this regard became increasingly significant. Interestingly enough, he had never been a member of a general agency before 1944. He had focused all his energies on local church, district, annual conference, and jurisdictional activities.

In his first quadrennium as a bishop he automatically became a member of the General Board of Education and of the Board of Missions, as were all the effective bishops residing in the United States. In his second quadrennium he was also a member of the Board of Temperance. In his last twelve years as bishop he served on the important Council on World Service and Finance, being the president from 1960 to 1968. He was called on for relatively minor roles while on the Board of Missions.

THE GENERAL BOARD OF EDUCATION

He served on the Board of Education for twelve years and became one of its most influential members, especially in the last eight years. During the first quadrennium of his membership, in the Division of the Local Church of the Board, he resumed relationships that went back nearly thirty years. The chairman of the division was Bishop Paul B. Kern, his seminary dean and friend. M. Leo Rippy, a fellow student from SMU, was the head of the division's adult work committee to which Bishop Martin was assigned. There were others on the board who were longtime or short-time associates: Merle T. Waggoner, layman from Wichita Falls, Floyd B. James of Ruston, Louisiana, and Ira A. Brumley of Conway, Arkansas, both from his own area; J. Earl Moreland from SMU days, Paul W. Quillian and J. N. R. Score from Texas, and of course, the other bishops from the South Central Jurisdiction.

During this twelve years on the Board of Education he served twice on the Committee on General Conference Legislation, both times being its chairman. For the last eight years he was a member of the Executive Committee.

As the 1948-52 quadrennium approached Dr. C. A. Bowen, executive secretary of the Editorial Division, and his administrative associate, Walter N. Vernon, proposed, and the board elected, Bishop Martin as the chairman of the Editorial Division. In those years it was the tradition that the chairman of the Editorial Division also served as chairman of the Curriculum Committee. These two responsibilities gave him the opportunity to influence the massive program of teaching resources that flowed into almost every local Methodist church. Dr. Leon M. Adkins of New York State served as the vice-chairman of the division; he also served on the Curriculum Committee.

During this quadrennium there were many currents flowing in regard to curriculum resources. On the one hand, circulation reached its highest point since Union in 1939, and the resources were greatly improved in content and appearance. On the other hand, many persons wrote critical letters to the editors—and some to Bishop Martin as the chairman. This was the era of McCarthyism, and many Methodists were harshly critical of any opinions that they felt were "soft on communism." Many expressions of social concern were placed in this category. Bishop Martin had to endure some letters generated by these feelings of fright over the changing positions of the church.

In an address to the Board of Education in January, 1952, the Bishop pointed out:

> One cannot imagine a more difficult task than the one that confronts this [curriculum] committee, the editors, their associates, and all other persons who have a part in producing our church-school literature.... Dr. Bowen, our able editor, in his report reminds us of two currents of interest which influenced the life of American Methodism—the desire to participate in political social action in the name of Christianity, and the conviction that the Christian Church finds its basic task in saving individuals and bringing about personal religious growth. The presentation of a proper balance between the varied emphases of the Christian gospel is no easy task.[1]

Another major issue to which Bishop Martin gave leadership in 1948-52 was a deadlock that had developed earlier over the issue of freedom of the editors of church school publications. The editors had a dual relationship—and responsibility; they were elected by the Board of Publication, having been nominated by the editor in chief, who was also an executive secretary of the Board of Education. The editors were "employees" of the Board of Publication and also staff members of the Board of Education. Some leaders felt the Board of Publication, by the power of election, or refusal to elect, could exercise undue control over the editorial content of curriculum resources. The issue had been taken to the General Conference in 1948.

The General Conference of 1948 created a special four-year commission to study this relationship of the Editorial Division to the two boards, and Bishop Martin was made its chairman. The solution that he and the commission developed, and that the General Conference of 1952 adopted, provided that the editors would not be elected by the Board of Publication, but would be appointed by the editor of church school publications. This system was followed until the drastic reorganization of boards in 1972.[2]

One story Bishop Martin delighted in telling from his Board of Education experience was about Mr. Morgan Stinemetz, art editor for church school publications:

> Mr. Stinemetz is a layman, but his associates call him "Deacon" since he

wears out more Bibles than anyone else in the Editorial Division. His accuracy caused him to question the popular painting of the *Rich Young Ruler* by Hoffman. In this painting the scene is indoors. Mr. Stinemetz discovered that the interview took place in the open road. This is why the interview between Christ and the rich young man is shown out of doors in our materials.[3]

In the 1948-52 quadrennium Bishop Martin participated in another important decision by the Editorial Division and the board: the election of a successor to Dr. C. A. Bowen, editor of church school publications. The decision narrowed to four persons: Dr. Leon M. Adkins, pastor and member of the board; Dr. Donald M. Maynard, curriculum writer and professor at Boston University School of Theology; Walter N. Vernon, who was administrative associate to Dr. Bowen and who had also served as secretary of the Curriculum Committee during Bishop Martin's chairmanship; and Dr. Henry M. Bullock, pastor at Jackson, Mississippi. Dr. Bullock was chosen by the committee and Bishop Martin nominated him to the board. He was elected and served for nearly twenty years in this position.

Three years later Bishop Martin was again chairman of a nominating committee to select a successor to Dr. John Q. Schisler as executive of the Division of the Local Church. The choice at that time was Dr. Leon M. Adkins, who had served with Bishop Martin on the Editorial Division and been considered as the editor. Bishop Martin had this latter responsibility because he was elected chairman of the Division of the Local Church in 1952. He is one of the few bishops—possibly the only one—ever to head two divisions of the Board of Education.

OTHER BOARDS

In the 1948-52 quadrennium Bishop Martin was called on to serve numerous agencies. In addition to the Boards of Education and Missions he was a member of the Board of Temperance (of which he was president), the Commission on World Peace, the Committee on Overseas Relief, and the Interboard Committee on Christian Vocations.

As president of the Board of Temperance Bishop Martin, in 1949, helped in the choice of a new executive secretary, Dr. Caradine Hooton, formerly a fellow member of the North Texas Conference. During the quadrennium several new features were developed, including a national meeting of the presidents of all conferences, a series of area seminars for area leaders, and a new type "School of Alcohol Studies and Christian

Action." The board was also challenged in this period regarding its tax-exempt status by the Internal Revenue Service. The board's argument was simply that we can "do no other than fight beverage alcohol in every possible way, including political and legislative activity. . . . It was our bounden religious duty." They won the argument![4]

In 1956 the bishop became a member of the Commission on Union, the Executive Committee of the World Methodist Council, and the Council on World Service and Finance. These last two agencies demanded more and more of his time until his retirement in 1968.

THE WORLD METHODIST COUNCIL

The World Methodist Council is committed to fostering unity, understanding, and fellowship among the Methodist bodies of the world. It has no legislative or administrative functions. It has a loose affiliation with the World Federation of Methodist Women and the International Association of Methodist Historical Societies. It arranges short-term exchange pastorates, chiefly between British and American pastors, sponsors institutes on Methodist theological studies, and arranges larger world-wide meetings at intervals of five or ten years.

Bishop Martin attended the Eighth Ecumenical Methodist Conference in Oxford, England in August-September, 1951. In 1956 he became chairman of Section XIII, which was made up of The Methodist Church in the United States, and thus he became also a member of the World Executive Committee.

During the Ninth World Methodist Conference, held in 1956 at Lake Junaluska, North Carolina, he participated in an unusual convocation in which many visiting Methodists were given degrees. He conferred the degree of Doctor of Laws on behalf of Centenary College upon the Rev. E. Benson Perkins, the secretary for the World Methodist Council for Great Britain, and upon Dr. Arthur Robert Hill, Senior Surgeon Consultant of Suffolk, England.

He was named to the program committee for the Tenth World Methodist Conference, held in Oslo, Norway in August, 1961, the theme for which was "New Life in the Spirit." Internationally known churchmen were in attendance, including non-Methodists such as Martin Niemöller and W. A. Visser 't Hooft. Bishop Martin was president of the Methodist Council of Bishops in 1961-62, and made one of the major addresses to the conference on the topic, "American Methodism since 1956." In the address he declared:

The Church of God has an opportunity to fulfill a decisive role in our generation. For it to be equal to its sacred responsibility there must be developed in its ministry leaders who are thoroughly aware of the sorry state of the world, who are critical of easy solutions and smug assumptions, who are sensitive to the frustrating sense of emptiness and dissatisfaction which characterize many people, who are courageous enough to sound a prophetic note which comes out of a holy boldness, who combine an evangelistic zeal, a social concern, and a crusading spirit and who proclaim a faith of world character and importance.[5]

Across these years many achievements were recorded in the World Methodist Council. The organization had two full-time secretaries of extraordinary zeal and imagination—E. Benson Perkins in Britain and Elmer T. Clark in the United States—and they brought the council to a period of rare accomplishments. The excellent headquarters building at Lake Junaluska was erected; over $60,000 was contributed in the United States to preserve and rehabilitate Epworth Rectory; significant worldwide sessions were held—some for serious theological consultation and some for inspiration and fellowship.

Three major publications were also an outgrowth of this period, not coming directly out of the council but stimulated by it through the International Association of Methodist Historical Societies. These were: the three-volume *Journal and Letters of Francis Asbury* (1958), published jointly by Abingdon Press in the United States and Epworth Press in Great Britain; *Who's Who in the Methodist Church* (1966), compiled by the editors of *Who's Who in America* and published by Abingdon Press; and the *Encyclopedia of World Methodism*, a mammoth undertaking and the first of its kind in over a century, to be published early in 1975 by Abingdon Press.

Perhaps most of all, Methodists from around the world were developing a deeper sense of oneness. This was helping the American Methodists shake off their provincialism. A second major value was accruing from the fact that numerous lay persons were being asked to become involved in the movement—and not merely for their monetary contributions.

PUBLICATIONS

"The Perils and Rewards of the Ministry" were the concerns Bishop Martin dealt with in a section of a booklet, *Young Men for Tomorrow's Ministry*. It was prepared by the bishop in 1951, and issued by the churchwide movement called the Advance for Christ and His Church. He listed four perils: (1) the peril of minimizing the greatness of the ministry,

(2) the danger of overambition, (4) the peril of laziness, and (4) the peril of being caught up in a round of good works.

He stressed the need for a minister to live a certain quality of life, and he listed as rewards: (1) the minister's own personal development, (2) the opportunity to stimulate others to high achievement, (3) the chance to interpret God to men, and (4) the opportunity to minister to persons at times of crucial experiences (birth, marriage, illness, death).

Humanity Hath Need of Thee is the title of a small devotional booklet by Bishop Martin. It has a subtitle, *Stories of Faith in Action*, and was published in 1957 by the General Board of Evangelism. It is made up chiefly of brief stories of persons who dared to stand by their convictions, even at severe cost.

OVERSEAS VISITATION

Among the many rich experiences the Martins have had have been the several trips overseas through which they have served the church. Several of these trips have been official "episcopal visitations" to learn about the work of Methodists in other lands. Others have been in line of duty in connection with the World Methodist Council and its predecessor bodies.

The first overseas trip, however, was made largely "on their own," and was a visit to the Holy Land. In addition to seeing Palestine, the Martins visited Egypt and Lebanon, as well as France, England, Italy, Austria, and Germany. In the latter country they attended the Passion Play at Oberammergau, a drama which was observing its 300th anniversary.

Bishop Martin has commented on some of his Methodist visitations overseas:

It was the Crusade for Christ program that took us to the Far East. Traveling by ship in company with Bishop and Mrs. Arthur J. Moore, who were going to Singapore, we visited Honolulu, Japan, Manila, Hong Kong, Formosa, Singapore, Penang, and India and Pakistan.

Tokyo provided an exciting Sunday dinner visit with General and Mrs. Douglas MacArthur.... Later in India we had similar visits with Prime Minister Nehru[6] and his daughter who is now the Prime Minister. Other leaders included Raj Kumari Amrit Kaur, Minister of Health; B. R. Ambedkar, Minister of Justice; and other important figures who also entertained us.

Traveling by train, plane, tonga, rickshaw, trishaw, jeep and even bullock cars, we had a heavy schedule during our two and a half months in India. There were only two free days for personal pursuits when we addressed cards to over 800 pastors back home. I dedicated countless churches as well as nine buildings of the Methodist Tuberculosis Hospital. I officiated at baptisms everywhere, once for 138 babies in a morning service at Hyderabad, and on another time baptizing an entire village.

This visit to India was the first of a succession of Episcopal visitations— one each quadrennium—to the mission fields of the church. There we familiarized ourselves with places, institutions, peoples and problems. Opportunities were provided to consult with church and national leaders. There were many public addresses.

A later visit took the Martins to South America. Among many events there Bishop Martin recalls this experience:

While in Argentina Bishop Sante Barbieri several times mentioned the need for workers to have automobiles to carry on their work. This was the time of the reign of the dictator, Juan Peron, and he would not allow them to be imported. I told the Bishop to advise me if the restrictions were lifted and I would try to secure some cars.

One morning I received an urgent cablegram. Peron had said the Methodists could import five cars, but the catch to it was they were to be shipped within the next two weeks. I did not see how it could be done, but another such offer might never come.

I called together some leaders of that wonderful Arkansas-Louisiana Area. I have never seen more ardent enthusiasm. Everyone cooperated; dealers made concessions. By the end of the week five preachers were driving shiny new Chevrolet and Ford cars to New Orleans to be loaded onto freighters.

Another such trip was to Africa. There were visits to many churches and missions, and rich experiences in seeing the Christian faith of the Africans. One humorous incident also stands out, as Bishop Martin tells it:

One morning at the Lomami River we found something had happened to the ferry boat. The only recourse left to us was a watu or hollowed-out log. The fear we already had was heightened by the knowledge that the river was infested with crocodiles. In the midst of the stream Mildred's hat was blown off. A crocodile lifted itself out of the water to devour it. Bishop Glenn Phillips, who with his wife was on a similar visitation, pinned on Mildred the title "The Queen of the Crocs."

Bishop Martin writes:

Wherever we went we were impressed by our schools and the interest shown in them. Particularly is this true in the Orient.

Outstanding educational institutions made possible by the Christian missionary enterprise are located in Korea. Best known perhaps is Ewha Woman's University, the largest one of its kind in the world. It was a thrilling sight to see 4,000 attractive girls in Chapel and to know the next day would bring another group as identical services had to be held to care for the 8,000 young women in the student body. The late Miss Helen Kim gave magnificent leadership there.

Other great leaders on these overseas trips come to mind. There were the Stevensons in India, the Don Waddells in Chile, Dr. and Mrs. Ernest Weiss in Korea, Dr. and Mrs. Herschel C. Aldrich in Madiad, India, Dr. and Mrs. Charles Perrill in India, Dr. and Mrs. William Hughlett and the Burleigh Laws of Africa, the David Lowerys in Chile, Helen Kim in Korea, John Yue, the tailor in Hong Kong, the Bishops, missionaries unnamed but not forgotten, and thousands of others who as we passed gave to us the only treasure they had, a smile of welcome.

The Episcopal visitation each quadrennium revealed to us opportunities for individuals, churches, districts, and conferences to assume support of missionaries and also to provide resources for buildings of various types and projects that would advance the cause of missions. While we were away we wrote letters for our conference papers and on our return we each spoke to groups and showed our pictures. Our people responded magnificently to the challenge.

JURISDICTIONAL ACTIVITIES

Service on numerous jurisdictional agencies took a good bit of Bishop Martin's time and energy. He met regularly with the Jurisdictional College of Bishops, and presided from time to time at the sessions of the Jurisdictional Conference.

He was a member, along with the other bishops of the South Central Jurisdiction, of such agencies as the Jurisdictional Council, Board of Education, Board of Missions, and Commission on Town and Country Work. He served for a time on the Commission on Finance, some of the time as its chairman. He was once chairman of the Jurisdictional Commission on Radio, and served on the Jurisdictional Conference Program Committee.

PRESIDING AT GENERAL CONFERENCE

Methodist bishops are most frequently seen nationally as they preside over sessions or carry out other duties at the General Conference. In fact, the favorite indoor sport of many General Conference delegates is to evaluate the ability of the various bishops to keep the conference on an even keel, out of parliamentary tangles, and relatively close to the planned agenda. This is not an easy task; there are parliamentary experts among the delegates; there are sharp intellects and brilliant speakers; and some of these are not averse to tripping up the presiding officers.

Bishop Gerald Kennedy revealed an attitude years ago that is probably shared by most of his colleagues; it was on the occasion of his first stint at presiding over the General Conference. The conference was dealing with a complicated issue—or at least it *got* complicated. In the midst of motions, amendments, and amendments to the amendment, one delegate asked Bishop Kennedy, "Bishop, may I move another amendment?" Bishop Kennedy, with his characteristic disarming air of an innocent in the midst of wolves, replied, "Yes, my brother, I think you can, but I sure hope you won't."[7]

Having been elected in 1944, Bishop Martin's first occasion for presiding was May 3, 1948, and then it was not at a business session but at an evening program session. However, he did conduct the memorial service for bishops and other members of the conference who had died. He revealed his ability to describe appropriately the bishops on the list that year:

No two of them are alike, but whether it be the contagious laughter of Bruce Baxter, the quiet dignity of Ernest Richardson, the untiring loyalty of Lorenzo King, the scholarly bearing of William Franklin Anderson, the ready enthusiasm of Schuyler Garth, the crusading zeal of James Cannon, Jr., the tested dependability of Friedrich Heinrich Otto Melle, the gracious thoughtfulness of John Lloyd Decell, the far-sighted statesmanship of John Lewis Nuelsen, or the missionary passion of John Wesley Robinson.[8]

In 1952 he presided at a business session of the conference; he was not called on in 1956; he presided again in 1960, 1964, and 1966. On all these occasions the sessions moved smoothly under his direction. When necessary he ruled motions out of order, or that no further discussion was allowable. He used a combination of courtesy and firmness; once in the midst of a count vote a delegate asked if amendments could be proposed if the vote did not carry. Bishop Martin jokingly replied, "I think that is a question that you should not have asked now," but then added, "I think you are privileged to ask it later."[9] On another occasion, as a standing count vote was being taken, he quipped, "It might be appreciated if we stand and sing 'I Shall Not Be Moved.' "[10]

Another time his geniality was revealed in a conference session in which it was proposed that $50,000 be allocated for the work of a new commission. Bishop Martin was called on to indicate whether this amount might be approved by the Council on World Service and Finance, of which he was chairman. He replied he would need a few minutes to confer with the treasurer. While doing so, the request was reduced to $20,000. Bishop Martin then said, "If they can reduce it so quickly I suggest we wait another hour." Then he added, "I believe we can provide the $20,000.00, and [with a chuckle] I think I ought to get a good deal of credit for saving the church $30,000.00."[11]

Bishop Martin was asked at the 1968 General Conference to respond on behalf of the bishops retiring that year, after they had been presented. He told one of his good stories, and then added: "At the close of this conference we will never have the right again to vote in the Council of Bishops but we *can* praise the Lord, and we are determined so to do. . . . We are grateful for a church . . . with a program that is great enough to challenge the most gifted person and simple enough to bless a little child."[12]

THE COUNCIL ON WORLD SERVICE AND FINANCE

In 1956 Bishop Martin was elected, along with Bishop G. Bromley Oxnam, to represent the Council of Bishops on the Council on World Service and Finance. Bishop Oxnam was elected president of the financial body, and Bishop Martin was named vice-president. Thus he had a good apprenticeship under one of the most dynamic Methodist bishops in this generation.

When the Council of Bishops voted on their representatives in 1960 to the World Service and Finance Agency, Bishop Martin was elected on the first ballot and Bishop Fred P. Corson on the second. Bishop Martin was subsequently elected president of the Council on World Service and Finance, and he continued his presidency until the time of his retirement in 1968.

The Council on Finance and Administration, as it is now designated, guides the general, or connectional, financial administration of the church. It recommends to each General Conference an amount to be set as the goal for churchwide giving; it develops the ratio on which this amount shall be apportioned among the several annual conferences and the thousands of local churches; it suggests the ratio on which the funds shall be divided among the general agencies (such as Missions, Discipleship, Higher Education, Social Concerns); it recommends the amount for salaries and pensions of the bishops; and it serves as a screening agency for groups appealing for additional funds between sessions of the General

Conference. Thus it ranks as one of the most influential and important agencies in the church.

During Bishop Martin's chairmanship several outstanding issues and innumerable tedious ones arose before the council.[13] The tedious ones, while of lesser scope than the outstanding ones, required careful attention and decision. Among examples of these were (1) requests from the National Council of Churches for additional funds for specific projects of the interdenominational body; (2) requests for additional funds for Methodist agencies (i.e. the Board of World Peace which had acquired a deficit, the Commission on Union, Methodist Information for coverage at the General Conference, the National Division of the Board of Missions to buy a church site in the Virgin Islands, Christian Social Concerns for a program at the Church Center at the United Nations, and special funding for studies about the attitudes and beliefs of Methodists); (3) requests for additional funds for pensions for overseas bishops, or their widows, or for travel funds for overseas bishops and/or their wives.

At one meeting, on November 8, 1965, the following requests were considered:

1. $25,000 for the Methodist bicentennial celebration
2. $50,000 for a study of the structure and work of the local church
3. $25,000 for 1965-66 and possibly $50,000 for the next two years for a young adult ministry
4. $25,000 to study the financial requirements of theological schools
5. $45,689 as additional support for the quadrennium of the Commission on Ecumenical Affairs
6. $3,000 additional funds each year in the quadrennium for the Commission on Worship
7. $15,000 in additional funds to help reduce the deficit on the Protestant Pavilion at the New York World's Fair
8. $5,000 for travel of overseas delegates to the World Methodist Conference/Council in London

Each of these concerns deserved—and received—careful consideration, and many of them received at least a part of the funds they requested.

Among the larger problems dealt with by the council have been two property debts. One has been the thorny issue of the purchase of the Wire Property, as it is called, in Washington, D.C. This desirable tract of nineteen acres in Northeast Washington, near American University, was originally purchased by the Board of Temperance in the 1950s as a likely location for housing all or many of the general agencies of the church. The Board of Temperance at that time had been led to believe by government officials that it might have to give up its building at 100 Maryland Avenue, N.E., and this new property offered a possible relocation site. However, the Board of Temperance overextended its resources in the purchase and came to the council on January 27, 1958, for emergency help on the matter. At the next meeting the council met in Washington (on April 14, 1958) and examined the property. The council, after examining all the facts, decided the Board of Temperance was able to handle the situation "for the present," but pointed out that the plan of financing it "is not comfortable financing. It greatly diminishes the liquidity of the investments of the Board of Temperance." The investigation revealed that carrying charges came to $80,000 a year, and that some other arrangement would be necessary.

In more recent years the Board of Christian Social Concerns (which incorporates now the assets and liabilities of the Board of Temperance) has faced financial difficulties because of the mortgage. On March 1, 1963, the council had a further report on the Wire Property, revealing that it still had a debt of $1,500,000, covered by three notes. The council, after reviewing the situation, reaffirmed its feeling that the property was a good investment, even if it was never used for church agency housing, but that funds from the church at large were needed to help finance it. An effort was made to secure monies through annual conferences, but no great amount was raised. In 1973 the financing of the property is still a problem, and its future use is unclear.

The second property problem has been in connection with the Church Center at the United Nations. At a special council meeting in Chicago on November 7, 1966, Dr. A. Dudley Ward, general secretary of the Board of Christian Social Concerns, reported that "the finances of the Board . . . involving specifically the Church Center for the United Nations, has brought this Board to a critical over-indebtedness and that funds for program were being used to cover building indebtedness." The council criticized itself for allowing situations to develop such as these "which are unsound." At the next meeting of the council, on March 30, 1967, it was reported that World Service funds and other operating funds had been comingled, that the indebtedness liabilities had not been correctly stated, and that the first mortgage under the current agreement was not self-amortizing. The council was told, however, that agreements had been worked out between the Board of Christian Social Concerns and the Woman's Division of the Board of Missions whereby the first mortgage would be amortized, and that at the end of twenty years the mortgages held by the Woman's Division would cover the present value of the building.

Upon Bishop Martin's retiring from the council, the Rev. Asbury Smith, a member of the council from the Baltimore Conference, spoke in appreciation of his service at a citation luncheon on April 20, 1968, in the Dallas Civic Auditorium. Referring to the bishop's birthplace, his first words were semihumorous:

Bishop Martin was born in Texas and has spent his entire ministry in this great State. There are 2,500 post offices with Zip Codes in this state, so Bishop Martin had a wide choice of places in which to be born. He could have been born in Egypt, Italy, Palestine, or the Klondike and still have been in Texas. He could have been born in London, Liverpool, or Paris and remained in Texas. Or he could have chosen Sunset, or, if this is not desired, Sunrise. He could have been born in Humble, Happy, or Loving. . . . He might have been born in Old Glory, Peacock, or Elysian Fields. He chose rather to be born in Blossom; this seems to me just right.

Then in more serious vein, Mr. Smith commented:

The Council has profited by your wide range of knowledge and wide experience. Your judgment has been uniformly good. We appreciate your gentle yet firm hand as presiding officer. I have seldom heard Bishop Martin laugh, but I always enjoy the little wrinkle about the lips that indicates he has just heard or is about to relate something humorous. This ready sense of humor has eased many tense situations.[14]

Bishop Martin himself expressed his feeling about the work of the council—and of the church—in the final report of the council under his presidency:

The work . . . [of] this great agency . . . has given me the coveted opportunity to see at close range the program of our church as it is not revealed in any other place. . . . World Service is the starting point for all Methodist benevolences, . . . the life blood for all Methodist benevolences, . . . the life blood without which the general boards cannot operate. . . . For 46 years now I have been a minister in The Methodist Church. I have never been more confident that my church may be used of God in a critical period in history. For such to be true there are some great needs. . . . We need a rebirth of loyalty to the church we love. . . . We need a fresh enthusiasm for our task. . . . We need a sense of unity in our church. World Service provides the only avenue through which that unity can be reached. . . . The acceptance of [World Service support] enthusiastically constitutes a glorious privilege, and a witness here may make possible for each of us a transforming experience.[15]

Bishop Martin's contribution to the leadership of general boards and agencies was made without a great deal of fanfare or glamour. It demanded much travel (domestic and worldwide), countless meetings, innumerable agenda, and resulted occasionally in snarls and difficulties. But it also involved being stimulated by personal contacts, wrestling with important issues, setting challenging goals, and evaluating the work of many agencies engaged in the work of the Kingdom.

CHAPTER ELEVEN

"Take Thou Authority to Preach the Word"

BISHOP PAUL V. GALLOWAY has said of Bishop Martin, "When Paul Martin stands in a pulpit to preach, he drops fifteen or twenty years from his age."[1] In essence, he was saying that preaching was something Bishop Martin enjoyed; it called forth his best effort.

Having authority and using authority are two different things. When ordained, a minister is declared by the bishop to have authority to preach the word of God. How well he or she exercises or uses this authority depends very much on the individual person.

Paul E. Martin's Paris High School English teacher (Miss A. D. Johns) had truly perceived his capacity to become a great speaker. In the School of Theology he had taken the course on homiletics, or sermon building, under Dr. Paul B. Kern, who was outstanding in his generation as a great educator, pastor, and bishop. The text for the course, *The Ministry to the Congregation*, was the standard one in Methodism for many years. It was written by the dean's father, John A. Kern.

What were the secrets of this excellent preaching? The chief among them may well be revealed in one of Paul Martin's own statements: "The final measure of one's true success as a minister depends on the inner certainty of his own soul." In all of his ministry he has been able to convey to his listeners this sense of his own unshakable faith in God. It is probably this ability that causes Dr. Hemphill Hosford to comment, "When he preached, he gave a sermon, not a lecture."

THOROUGH PREPARATION

Paul Martin early set for himself a high standard in preaching. He was determined that he would always be thoroughly prepared whenever he was to speak or preach. He had an amazing capacity to meet this high standard—even when called upon to speak on short notice. Before he was elected bishop the problem was not so great, as the times for preaching were usually well established and known ahead of time. But after he became a bishop he was increasingly called on to speak on short notice or very frequently at times when the pressure of other duties occupied him day and night. But the most universal testimony among his acquaintances is that he had always prepared especially for the particular occasion involved. This trait reveals his sense of the importance of the message he was communicating—and the significance of the persons to whom he was speaking.

WRITING OUT SERMONS

Bishop Martin carefully wrote out most of his sermons ahead of time, but he did not read from the papers when presenting them to his congregation. He was able to deliver them essentially as he had written them, without being tied to the manuscript.

"Umphrey Lee told me one time he always wrote out what he had to say," writes Dr. Hemphill Hosford. "Both Umphrey and Paul [Martin] had the ability to give a talk or sermon—using the written page—but never giving one the impression they had it written out. Paul told me once he was not sure you could teach one this art."[2] Such an ability gives a speaker the double advantage of both careful structure and freedom of delivery.

In his writing he was a master at fashioning expressive and appropriate phraseology. A few examples will indicate this:

We Americans specialize in the impossible. We Christians proclaim, "we can do all things through Christ who strengtheneth us."

No man needs to be sure of everything. It is enough that he be sure of something.

Goodness is unmistakable like the perfume of the rose.

Responsiveness to human need is the prime test of discipleship.
One reason why indifference is so deadly is that it never seems so deadly.

ILLUSTRATIONS FROM WIDE SOURCES

In addition to his own expressive phrases, he drew widely on other speakers and writers for stories, incidents, sayings, and ideas to enrich his messages. Poetry and drama, fiction and history, philosophical and theological studies, the daily newspapers, and the daily conversations—all were scanned for pertinent and graphic comments on life, on humankind, on the state of religion, on the meaning of religion and life, on the relation between man and God.

The following list of sources for a single sermon reflects the wide range of ideas and illustrative material he drew upon:[3] St. Augustine, Harnett T. Kane, the *New York Herald Tribune*, Mark Twain, Vice-Admiral Rickover, the Gospel according to St. Luke, the *New York World Telegram*, William L. Stidger, Alfred Lord Tennyson, 1 John, James Russell Lowell, Ralph Waldo Emerson, G. A. Studdert-Kennedy, Alfred Noyes, and Pierre Lecomte du Noüy.

A few examples will illustrate one type of quotation he used—the apt phrase that added spice, as it were, to the already rich fruitcake:

A preacher never runs out of soap, [but] sometimes he can't make it lather.
The recipe for compounding many a current sermon might be written: "Take a teaspoon of weak thought, add water, and serve."
He knew all the little answers, but he missed the large questions.
They know all the four letter words except soap.
Great occasions do not make heroes or cowards; they simply unveil them to the eyes of men.

One might think that the use of many illustrations and quotations would create a disunity, but their use is always made subservient to the message of the sermon. So skillfully are they woven together that there is no threat to the thought flow. Less able preachers sometimes fall into the error of using so many illustrations that the basic message is lost. This is especially likely to happen if the speaker is concerned too greatly with being popular and well-liked. Every sermon, in Dr. Martin's judgment, ought to be interesting enough to command the attention of his listeners, but it does not necessarily have to be popular. He took to heart the admonition of that other most interesting yet most profound pulpiteer of Texas Methodism, Umphrey Lee (and a good friend of Martin's from the opening years at SMU), who always maintained that "no preacher has a license to be dull."[4]

While in his wide reading he evidently read from the works of some of the more modern scholars—among them Niebuhr, Bultmann, Tillich, Outler, Brunner—it is noteworthy that he quoted from them directly only occasionally. Whatever use he made of the ideas of the scholars was done chiefly after interpretation and "translation" into his own language. This approach shows his sensitivity to the needs of his hearers, and his recognition of the fact that lay persons (and many preachers?) may not be entirely familiar with technical theological language.

SERMONS BASED ON SIMPLE, PROFOUND TRUTHS

He concentrated in his sermons on simple yet profound truths, a trait copied from the sermons and teachings of the Master Teacher, Jesus Christ. This approach enabled him to speak to "the man in the pew," and to be understood and have influence. We have noted this passion for developing and maintaining close personal relationships with almost all the persons he knew. As a result he was aware of feelings and frustrations, hopes and fears, joys and sorrows, likes and dislikes of all sorts of people. This was reflected in the content of his preaching.

He never scolded or condemned—even in the name of the Lord. Rather, before a congregation he lifted up the Lord God Almighty in all his beauty and holiness. Then he called upon each individual to find there the inspiration for a pattern of holy living and holy dying.

In line with this emphasis on simple, profound truths we are not surprised to find that Paul Martin's sermons are invariably rooted in biblical incidents, stories, and teaching. He makes use of a biblical text, and frequently includes references to biblical events and messages. All of the sermons in the series, "Life's Opposites," are built upon biblical situations. In these sermons he draws sharp contrasts between good and evil, or between other aspects of life's meaning. Sermon titles in this series include "Two Towns" (Sodom and Jerusalem), "Two Gardens" (Eden and Gethsemane), "Two Ways to Be Remembered" (avoiding responsibility or accepting it), "Two Men on Crosses" (one on either side of Jesus on the cross), "Two Last Suppers" (Belshazzar's feast and Jesus' Last Supper), and "Night or Day?" (Judas going out into the night of betrayal, and the risen Christ and the dawn).

The down-to-earth titles in another sermon series are "Face Washing" (going forth to meet life with all its difficulties and in spite of obstacles),

"Hand Washing" (seeking to absolve ourselves from our own wrong-doings), and "Foot Washing" (taking on the servant role).

His Voice and Delivery

The delivery of a sermon can be as important as its preparation. On this score Paul Martin was blessed with an excellent voice—and he made excellent use of it.

The tone of his voice is clear, resonant, and deep, but not too deep to be easily heard. He has complete control of it; he never stammers or stumbles, never lets it wander off into extreme heights or depths, but keeps it well within a pleasing range for the listener. It is never monotonous because he is able to produce emphasis and variety and expressiveness with only the slightest of variations in his manner of speaking. The liveliness in his voice is a match for the twinkle in his eye. He gives credit to Miss Mary McCord, speech and drama professor at SMU, for guidance in his speech patterns.

His delivery can be characterized as conversational, rather than oratorical, yet it is not casual. It has an earnestness and at times an intensity of feeling that makes it clear that the speaker is deadly serious about his message. He grew up, of course, in a time when preaching was generally of the oratorical type. Undoubtedly he discovered early, through his experiences in drama and debate, how to project a message with force without having to shout—or to pound on the pulpit, another fairly common technique of earlier days. At the same time, his pulpit manner is one of openness and geniality, serious but never gloomy. His mood is almost invariably one of hopefulness, rooted in the joy the Christian finds in fellowship with God.

Mr. Charles Prothro of Wichita Falls has observed that one "secret of Bishop Martin's success in the pulpit [is that] he speaks slowly and distinctly, and that gives his hearers time to digest what he is saying."[5] This is an important element; but at the same time his delivery is not so slow as to make the message drag. There is a liveliness in his voice, and occasional flashes of humor that bring chuckles and sometimes laughs.

The Message of His Sermons

What is the basic message that he has emphasized in his sermons across the years? It is that man is a creature in need of God's grace and forgiveness; that God offers His grace and forgiveness freely through the sacrifice of Jesus Christ; that the Christian life demands "mighty purposes, great faiths, compelling loyalties, and powerful compulsions . . . [to] press forward to no less than the attainment of the high calling of Jesus Christ our Lord."

He declared that some tragedies may be unexplainable, but that "in the center of them is to be found a God of love, offering to his children unseen, infinite resources. . . . You may not be able to explain tragedy but you can triumph over it. . . . God does not interrupt the course of nature with miraculous interference. . . . But steadily and surely God works within human minds and hearts to bring His purpose to the world."

The Christian life, he maintains, is not an easy road along which we simply accept God's grace and then drift indolently toward Heaven. He points out that in several of the parables (the Good Samaritan, the Talents) Jesus stressed the responsibility that each person has. "Most of us know that many things are wrong today, but for fear of losing friends, or of being ridiculed as narrow and puritanical, we do not take a positive stand against them."

While he recognized man's sinful nature (no pastor who goes in and out of homes can fail to do so) he stoutly maintained that "one of the distinctive marks of Christianity is that it teaches men to hold a lofty opinion of themselves and of their fellow men. They are children of God, made in his image, destined for his character."

His Rank as Preacher

Due to the circumstances of his life, Paul E. Martin has probably not been ranked as high as he deserves, denominationally and nationally, as a preacher. Church folks have a tendency to praise even poor preaching. But among those who have ranked Bishop Martin's preaching as excellent are a number of competent judges.

Here are several comments on his preaching—and none made by persons who were looking for an appointment or other favor:

Bishop Paul V. Galloway (July, 1963): "I have never seen a preacher at any [Texas] Pastors School received with such appreciation and love. I am now asking the Lord to let it rub off on me."

Dr. Charles Allen (May 15, 1966): "Your sermon last Sunday stands out in my mind as one of the few really great sermons I have ever heard. It is the only sermon I have ever heard preached on music in the church."

Bishop A. Frank Smith (February, 1951): "Your thought, your words, your handling of the entire situation was superb. You can always rise to any occasion, but this time you jumped completely over it.

"I must say I have never heard any man preach with greater force and to better advantage than you did there [Texas Pastor's School, 1954]."

Bishop Richard C. Raines: "The years have simply deepened and enriched your ability to stimulate. . . . I especially honor the flexibility and up-to-dateness of your mind and spirit."

Dr. J. Henry Bowdon: "He was a great preacher . . . in the spiritual force of his personality and the easy flow of his language . . . I believe that Bishop Martin would number among the ten greatest preachers among all the [over 200 Methodist] bishops we have ever had. He was real and genuine . . . sincere and honest in his messages."

Bishop William C. Martin (Fall, 1972): "I have never heard him when he did not give a very interesting, very helpful, and constructive sermon. He made about the best use of anybody I know of contemporary drama, literature, and current plays for illustrative material for his sermons."

"Making the sermon," wrote Bishop John M. Moore, "is absolutely the prerequisite to making the preacher. St. Paul wrote to Timothy, 'Attend to your scripture reading, your preaching, your teaching.' The man who does that faithfully will not be dull or dispersive, and the man who does it will not be unprofitable."[6]

As one looks on the entire life span of the ministry of Paul E. Martin, it appears that not only his preaching but his whole life's impact on persons was aimed at calling forth the best in them through goodwill, love, encouragement, praise—and challenge. "The great opportunity of the Christian Church," he declared, "is to create an expectancy across the earth. . . . Triumph awaits transformed men and women who contemplate the glorious future God has set before them and in complete abandon give themselves to its realization in the lives of men. We are not blind, defeated, plodding slaves, but a company of men who are heirs of God."

CHAPTER TWELVE

"Alma Mater We'll Be True, Forever"

BISHOP PAUL E. MARTIN has had longer and closer contact with Southern Methodist University, and especially with Perkins School of Theology, than any other one person, except for Mrs. John H. Warnick, who for many years has served as librarian and as bibliographic expert to students and faculty alike.

His first contacts with the theological side of the university began almost from the time he entered SMU as a freshman in 1915. The university was small, and most of the students were Methodists. Bible courses were required; chapel attendance was compulsory. Attendance at the university church, Highland Park Methodist, was almost universal. There was a much greater sense of denominational unity in the student body than is possible now in a large, cosmopolitan, pluralistic university.

Consequently, undergraduates and theologs were much more closely associated then than they have been, generally speaking, in more recent years. They participated in a great many of the campus activities, particularly those sponsored by the YMCA and the YWCA. Because the faculty was smaller in those days, the theological professors were more widely known to the student body.

Following his three years of teaching at Blossom, Paul Martin entered the School of Theology for a three-year period. Here he formed deep and lasting friendships among the professors and students. Many of his classmates have been among the leaders in the Methodist church across the years of his ministry.

NAMED A TRUSTEE

In 1934, less than ten years after he left the seminary, Dr. Martin was named by the North Texas Conference as one of its representatives to the Board of Trustees of Southern Methodist University. This membership continued officially for thirty-four years, until the time of his retirement in 1968. Since then he has continued to serve the university, for a time as a faculty member and later as adviser and consultant to Dean Quillian.

Dr. Martin attended his first trustees' meeting on January 29, 1935.[1] Present at that meeting of the board were three bishops, twelve ministers, and seven laymen. About this time, however, an advisory committee of laymen was created, and eventually the lay members came to outnumber the clergy.

At this first meeting a policy was established "that only persons of known Christian character, actively related to some Christian church or congregation should be employed as teachers, or as officials in the administration of this institution." The policy also required that "directing heads, and a majority of the entire staff be active members of the church sponsoring the institution." This was not surprising in view of the fact that (according to a report of President Charles C. Selecman two years later) the student body consisted of 785 Methodists, with only 238 Baptists, 196 Presbyterians, 106 Episcopalians, 103 Disciples, 92 Catholics, 60 Jews, 18 Christian Scientists, and a scattering of others.

During the three years Dr. Martin was in charge of the Wichita Falls District (1935-1938), Mr. and Mrs. J. J. Perkins of Wichita Falls made the first of their many generous gifts to the university. In January of 1937 they contributed $5,000 in the campaign to reduce the university's current indebtedness. On June 7, 1938, President Selecman announced to the trustees that he had received a much larger gift of $75,000 from the Perkinses to finance the addition of the second and third stories to the one-story, unfinished administration building. The completed building was dedicated on February 7, 1939, with Dr. Martin participating in the dedication service.

Encouraging Giving

When Dr. Martin became pastor of First Church, Wichita Falls, in the fall of 1938, he was instrumental in encouraging Mr. and Mrs. Perkins, Mr. J. S. Bridwell, and other Wichita Falls citizens to invest in the future of Southern Methodist University. Mr. Perkins agreed to serve as a member of the executive committee and of the budget committee in 1939, and Mr. Bridwell became a member of the board in 1940. Mr. W. B. Hamilton had been connected with the board beginning in 1928. Dr. Martin was named to the board's Committee on Instruction and its Committee on the School of Theology in 1938.

One delicate task to which Dr. Martin gave the benefit of his ameliorating spirit related to a long-felt and strongly-expressed need to strengthen the seminary's courses in Christian education and the work of the local church. For many years Dr. James Seehorn Seneker had taught all these courses. Original, prophetic, and unique, he was a loyal devotee of George Albert Coe, professor at Union Theological Seminary, under whom he had studied. Some of Dr. Seneker's mannerisms caused many students to avoid his courses; as a result, the congregations they later served were deprived of the practical help needed in the program of Christian nurture. In 1944 Dr. Martin worked with the small board committee that developed a plan to bring in a professor to deal with practical aspects of local church education. Dr. Seneker was allowed to continue the contribution for which he was suited in the area of theory and philosophy of Christian education.

Honored by the University

By 1945 the university acknowledged that Bishop Paul E. Martin ought to be recognized in a special way for his contribution to the advancement of the Christian faith and the Christian church. Consequently, at the 1945 commencement he was awarded the honorary degree of Doctor of Laws. The citation read when he was presented for the degree described him in these words: "Successful pastor; tolerant, understanding, wise administrator of the Church's spiritual and temporal affairs; statesmanlike in helping build and direct institutions of welfare and education; by election Bishop in the Church of God."

Dr. Martin has pointed out that the moral backing of influential laymen on the board of trustees has strengthened the hand of the university administration. This was particularly evident on one occasion when the beer dealers' association of Dallas offered generous gifts of money to some of the Dallas schools, including SMU. Bishop Martin writes:

There was some hesitation in the acceptance. Finally Mr. J. S. Bridwell and Mr. J. J. Perkins called the President. "What are you going to do about that beer money?" he was asked. "We will wait for action by the Board of Trustees," was the reply. "Why are you waiting? Tell them we don't want their money!" I am firmly convinced that had that money been accepted, certain great gifts would never have been made. In a day when there is so much vacillating in moral matters, it is refreshing to remember that two laymen sounded a convincing note.

"A RARE MUNIFICENT GIFT"

Undoubtedly the most significant and far-reaching event in SMU history with which Paul E. Martin was connected was the providing of funds by his close friends, Joe J. and Lois Perkins, for a substantial endowment and a complete new complex of buildings for the School of Theology. Bishop John M. Moore, who had previously served as chairman of the board of trustees for many years, called this "a rare, munificent, and magnificent gift." The influence of Bishop Martin in this decision of the Perkinses to make such a splendid gift can hardly be overestimated; Mrs. Perkins has said that much of Mr. Perkins's giving to church causes was inspired by Bishop Martin.

While the idea for such a gift had been conceived earlier, it did not materialize until 1944. Bishop Martin, who at that time had been the Perkins's pastor for six years, gives this account of the decision:

The matter had been under discussion for some time, and on Tuesday afternoon, June 13, 1944, following the afternoon session of the Jurisdictional Conference [in Tulsa], a group met in the hotel room of Mr. and Mrs. Perkins. . . . In addition [to the Perkinses] were Dr. Umphrey Lee, Bishop A. Frank Smith, Mildred [Mrs. Martin], and I. . . . This was the time in which the project definitely came into being, although the announcement was not made until several months later. . . . This meeting that afternoon in the Mayo Hotel in Tulsa was of great significance.[2]

A friend once asked Mr. Perkins why he chose the School of Theology on which to bestow their millions, rather than the School of Business or the School of Law. He replied, "Because I believe the future will be determined by the ministry of the church."[3] At another time he wrote:

"If through the years we could be helpful in developing through this agency just one Paul Martin and one Mildred Martin, we would feel . . . well repaid."[4] At the suggestion of Mr. Perkins, one of the dormitories—an apartment for young married couples in the quadrangle—was named Paul E. Martin Hall.

The original gift (announced in February, 1945) for the School of Theology was $1,350,000; but Mr. and Mrs. Perkins have given substantially in excess of $10,000,000 to the school that bears their name. Two buildings in the quadrangle were given by others: Kirby Hall, a gift of Harper and Annie Kirby of Austin, and Bridwell Library, a gift of Mr. J. S. Bridwell and daughter, Margaret, of Wichita Falls.

Enlarging the Perkins Campus

After the gift for new facilities was received, plans were made to erect the new buildings around the one building already in use, Kirby Hall (now Florence Hall, a part of the Law Quadrangle). However, Bishop John M. Moore, retired but still active in the affairs of the university, became convinced that a new location was needed. On August 23, 1947, he wrote to Bishop Martin about this concern:

I am distressed at the possibility of building on that four acres, making crowded . . . quarters. To me it would be almost a disaster. What would our preachers and our church think of us 25 years from now? We have the opportunity of building a great plant on a great campus of fascinating prominence and possibility. We must not throw it away. We are building for a hundred years, for a great church, for a great Methodist ministry. I believe Mr. Perkins would see the greatness of the 21-acre plot. We must do all we can to help him and Mrs. Perkins to see it. You can do a lot. Be sure to do it and soon.[5]

Soon Bishop Moore called the Martins in Little Rock and asked them to come to Dallas immediately. Bishop Martin reports on that meeting:

With an architect's skill he had drawn two sets of plans. One set demonstrated that the future would be limited in the old location.

The other plan carefully drawn to scale pointed out the use of the land, then known as Arden Forest, where the school is now located, and placed the buildings almost exactly where they now stand.

After he had carefully explained the matter, he took me by the hand and said, "Paul and Mildred, you are the ones who can make this possible. Umphrey Lee and Eugene Hawk do not agree with me. You must go this afternoon to Wichita Falls. Mr. and Mrs. Perkins will listen to you. Show them these plans. Point out to them the limitations of the ground which is now being considered. This is perhaps the most important opportunity that has ever come to you."

That afternoon his plans were spread out on a table. Mr. Perkins immediately perceived the limitation of the one plan as in contrast with Bishop Moore's suggestions. When he spoke he said, "Bishop Moore is right. I will call Umphrey Lee in the morning."

Mr. Perkins not only called Dr. Lee but wrote Bishop Moore on September 7, as follows:

Mrs. Perkins and I have talked with various interested parties. After thinking this matter over carefully, I am not sure but that you are correct. . . . If the Theological School is placed on this four-acre plot it would seem that it would be equivalent to saying to the public . . . that we never expect this school to be any larger.[6]

Mrs. Perkins added a note of her own to Bishop Moore's in which she expressed a wish: "I want the chapel to be where it can be seen, and the center of all the other buildings." Bishop Moore wrote the Martins about the letter from the Perkinses, and expressed his approval of her suggestion by adding "Fine! Fine! Fine!" in his letter. And then he said, "You have done a magnificent work. . . ." When the Martins returned to Dallas, their meeting with Bishop Moore was heartwarming. Bishop Martin wrote: "Our return to the Bishop's home provided one of the most touching experiences we have ever known. The frail old man took me in his arms as a father would his son. 'Paul, this is one of the most significant moments I have ever had. I can now die happy. God bless you!' "[7]

The plans were soon perfected and building got under way. The original plans called for a chapel, a classroom building, and two dormitories. As further thought was given to the needs of the school, these plans were expanded eventually to include nine buildings: Perkins Chapel, Kirby Hall (office and classroom building, named for the original Kirby Hall that was left in the Law Quadrangle), five dormitories—John M. Moore Hall, Paul E. Martin Hall, A. Frank Smith Hall, Eugene B. Hawk Hall, and Sam B. Perkins Hall, an office and assembly hall named Charles C. Selecman Hall (containing a Lois Perkins Auditorium), and Bridwell Library, a gift of other members of First Church, Wichita Falls, Mr. J. S. Bridwell and his daughter, Margaret.

The impact of the Perkins's gift was significant not only because it provided the physical plant that was erected but perhaps even more because it made possible the expansion of the faculty. Salaries were increased, enabling the school to attract professors with national and international reputations—or professors of such a caliber that they achieved excellent reputations after coming to the school. The SMU School of Theology gradually became one of the great seminaries of the church and nation.

SOME UNEVEN STRETCHES

The progress of the school was not without its uneven stretches. One of these came in 1950 and 1951. Bishop Martin again played a key role in the situation, according to his "Reflections":

In November, 1950, the Board of Trustees with hearty approval (Mr. Perkins spoke in its favor when the issue was before the Board) decided to admit Negroes to the school as regular students, to attend the classes of their choice, and to receive credit. For a time all went well. Then some of the Negroes were invited by white students to share rooms with them. Then a potentially explosive problem arose when some members of the Board of Trustees took the position that it was never intended that they should room together in the dormitories. The atmosphere became tense. Understandably, Mr. Perkins was worried because of the pleas made to him by some of the trustees.

The authors of *Umphrey Lee: A Biography* (Winifred T. Weiss and Charles S. Proctor) said: "The situation became most difficult since three key people, best placed to smooth out difficulties, were temporarily unavailable. Bishop Paul E. Martin, Chairman of the Trustees' Committees of Perkins School of Theology, was overseas; the wife of Bishop A. Frank Smith, chairman of the Board of Trustees, had suffered a serious heart attack which held him close to Houston; President Lee had suffered a heart attack and was for a time unavailable."

Then I returned from the overseas visitation. Bishop Smith, President Lee, and Dean Merrimon Cuninggim convinced me that they believed I could help to resolve the difficult situation. My wife and I spent part of the Christmas holidays in Wichita Falls with our dear friends. One evening Mr. Perkins, in the direct fashion that always characterized him, asked me, "Do you believe that if this matter is not settled in an amicable manner, it will hurt the University?" I replied in the affirmative. Then he simply but sincerely said, "That is the only consideration. The University must rise above any hurt feelings that can develop. The School of Theology is our first love."

Bishop A. Frank Smith in his report on the settlement of this issue said that it was referred to the Committee on the School of Theology, of which Bishop Martin was chairman. The matter was considered at a meeting with Mr. and Mrs. Perkins present. Mrs. Perkins took the position that the students were hurting no one by being in the dorms, and the committee agreed to let matters stand as they were.[8]

Bishop Martin, as Chairman of the Trustees Committee of the Perkins School of Theology from 1944 to 1968, held this important post through the significant years of expansion; and they were years of occasional turbulence and constant excitement.

In November, 1953, the board of trustees selected Bishop Martin as one of its distinguished alumni, on nomination of the Alumni Association. The award was presented in March, 1954. The committee making the selection was composed of Eugene McElvaney, Bishop William C. Martin, S. J. Hay, Ross Priddy, and Gerald C. Mann. The citation presented with the award made clear his achievements and qualities of life, and commended Dr. Martin for his "personal attainment, his public service, and [the] honor that he has reflected upon his University by his character and work."[9]

A TRIBUTE TO J. J. PERKINS

On September 14, 1960, after several years of ill health, Mr. Joe J. Perkins reached the end of his earthly life. Bishop and Mrs. Martin were at the side of the Perkins family, bringing to them personal support and the comfort of the Christian faith. At the meeting of the board of trustees on November 4, Bishop Martin read a resolution of appreciation for Mr. Perkins. Their esteem for each other grew out of their long association and close personal relationship; and much of their time together was spent on behalf of the university. The resolution reflected this relationship:

The magnificent benefactions of Mr. Perkins were no more noteworthy than his outstanding personal qualities derived from the nobility of his character. . . . He was a successful business man, a generous philanthropist, a good citizen, a consecrated Christian, a devoted husband and father, and beloved neighbor and friend. . . .

It is altogether appropriate that on this occasion when this Board pauses to pay tribute to this great Christian gentleman, his wife is officially seated as a member of the group. She has ably represented him during his illness at our meetings. He never made the presentation of any gift without saying "I have often made the statement that I never had a good intention that my wife did not bear me out 100 per cent. Sometimes I suggest a gift; sometimes she finds a cause; but we always work together and get a thrill out of the results."

Southern Methodist University will always be aware of his generosity and forever grateful for the life of Joseph J. Perkins.

Bishop Paul E. Martin and Mr. Perkins were very close friends; each had high respect and affection for the other. Each achieved a high position in his chosen field; each used his particular talents for the tasks that he could do best. Each contribute 1 in a monumental way to the welfare of Southern Methodist University.

A PHILOSOPHY FOR THEOLOGICAL EDUCATION

The philosophy on which Bishop Martin formed his judgments regarding the direction for theological education is revealed in these words from his "Reflections":

In every field of learning today the need is for hard, straight, fearless thinking. Particularly is that true in the realm of religion. An atomic space age demands a new understanding, a deeper grasp of, and a fresh insight into, the eternal verities. Our young ministers must be led into the most thorough intellectual disciplines. They must be prepared for clear, honest, critical thinking. They must gain insight into the meaning and application of the Christian faith for their responsibility of communicating the truth to others. It is a difficult day in which to preach the gospel of Christ and to make it the dominating force—which it must be if the world is to be saved. No man can be equal to his responsibility who is not adequately prepared for his holy task.

As I think of the years spent in the Seminary I am reminded of a tremendously impressive address by a ninety-five-year-old man, Bishop Herbert Welch, at the dedication of the chapel at Wesley Theological Seminary. In his message he asked a question concerning the students, "What do they most need?" and proceeded to answer first by discussing the relationship between the student and his faculty.

"These theologians are reasonably mature; they have passed the crisis of doubt, they have opinions which may indeed already have hardened into convictions. But they still need counselors, they still need understanding. In a word, there will probably never be a time in their unfolding lives when human fellowship will be more important and more welcome than in this preparatory stage. The library, even the chapel, will not take the place of the human touch.

"We must have scholars, for competence is as necessary here as elsewhere. We must have good teaching lest scholarship become dry as dust and students gain no love of learning. But one would be disappointed in an instructor who kindled no flame, or at least struck no spark of interest, curiosity or intellectual enthusiasm in the minds of those who sat under his instruction.

"But we need more than a pedant or a drill master. The fact of the case is that a theological course should find its chief justification for the time and money it costs in affording intimate contacts with a few great personalities. Our continuous contact with Jesus Christ is the very source of our salvation. Contact with the good and the great may determine a life's direction, its ideals, its growth; and the quality of a faculty will largely decide whether a school shall be distinguished or mediocre."

As I stand often in that magnificent Perkins quadrangle I think it is a far cry from the cramped quarters of the third floor of Dallas Hall to the present luxurious buildings, beautifully located, but I pray that today's students may find something of the transformation that came to my life, almost a half a century ago. How grateful I am to have known Hoyt N. Dobbs, Paul B. Kern, Robert W. Goodloe, Comer Woodward, James Seehorn Seneker, President Charles C. Selecman, John H. Hicks, James Kilgore, W. D. Bradfield, Harvie Branscomb, and others.

In more recent years Bishop and Mrs. Martin have been funding for the university the Paul and Mildred Martin Endowed Scholarship. It now amounts to almost $30,000.

The record gives ample evidence of the loyalty and commitment of Paul E. Martin to the highest standards for university and theological education—and to Southern Methodist University and Perkins School of Theology, two of the prime agencies for bringing about such education. He has not sought to deal with administrative operations of the university, but has centered on larger concerns, such as competent faculty, comprehensive curriculum, freedom for theological interpretation, adequate facilities, and an understanding of the school's role by the church and the general public. He has provided frequent counsel and support, occasional cautions, rare warnings, and constant assurances of his readiness to give time and energy to meet the needs of the school to which, in one sense, he has given his life.

Dean Joseph D. Quillian, Jr. has assessed Bishop Martin's contribution to the school in these terms:

Bishop Paul was easy to talk with as chairman of the Trustees Committee. He was considerate and insightful in giving advice, always accompanied by encouragement. As a member of the Perkins staff, he is a close personal friend as well as advisor and confidant. It means much to me personally as well as professionally to have the affectionate colleagueship of the man who was chief inspiration for the school that I serve.

CHAPTER THIRTEEN

Retrospect

WHEN THE BOARD OF TRUSTEES of Southern Methodist University met in November, 1968, special reference was made to several members who were retiring, among whom were Bishops W. Angie Smith and Paul E. Martin. President Willis M. Tate and Chairman Eugene McElvaney made appropriate statements about the retiring trustees and expressed the hope that the two bishops, especially, would continue to be interested in and helpful to the university. At that point Bishop Smith arose and said, "Mr. Chairman, I don't know anything that is deader than a retired bishop."

Since President Tate had mentioned that Bishop Martin, though retired, was to do some teaching at Perkins School of Theology, Bishop Martin retorted to Bishop Smith, "Well, it's going to be different this time."[1] And it has been a busy time for Bishop and Mrs. Martin since his retirement in 1968.

RETIREMENT EVENTS

There were many retirement events. In addition to the recognition given retiring bishops at the General Conference of 1968, at which

124

Bishop Martin responded for all, there was a warm address of appreciation by Dr. Alfredo Nanez at the Rio Grande Conference dinner. The
Texas Conference dedicated a session of the annual conference to Bishop
and Mrs. Martin, and it was at this session that an anthem, composed for
the occasion by Lloyd Pfautsch, was played, and Bishop William C.
Martin spoke. The Jurisdictional Conference in Oklahoma City then
honored Bishop Martin and Bishop Smith at a dinner, with Dr. Willis
M. Tate as toastmaster.

On Wednesday, February 7, 1973, the annual Ministers' Week
Luncheon at SMU was the occasion for honoring the life and labors of
Bishop and Mrs. Paul E. Martin. At its close, Bishop Martin said, "This
will always be one of the great days of our lives." The luncheon featured
brief tributes by Dean Joseph D. Quillian, Jr., Dr. J. Kenneth Shamblin,
Mr. Charles Prothro (speaking also for Mrs. J. J. Perkins), and Dr.
James E. Brooks (speaking for President Paul Hardin and Chancellor
Willis M. Tate of the university). Two special choir numbers, both
especially written by Lloyd Pfautsch and Carlton Young in Bishop Martin's honor, were sung by the University Choir and by the Seminary
Singers. It was a time of close, warm fellowship between many persons,
some of whom had known the Martins since days of childhood and youth.

Retired but Active

In February, 1968, Bishop Martin was invited by the late Dr. William
H. Dickinson to "occupy the Highland Park Church [Dallas] pulpit for
an extended period." Dr. Dickinson was to take a leave of absence. After
considering the invitation carefully Bishop Martin replied, "We sincerely
believe we cannot accept the invitation at this time."[2] He felt he was due
—and needed—a chance to relax and rest without regular heavy responsibilities.

He had already accepted an invitation to teach and counsel at Perkins
School of Theology for the 1968-72 quadrennium. He found this a satisfying task, for he was associated with the school he loved so much and to
which he had given so much. He enjoyed having an office at the school,
and enjoyed the contacts with professors and students. He comments thus
in his own words:

The relationship to Perkins School of Theology has been one for which
I have been most grateful. I am convinced more than ever that if Mr.
Perkins were alive, he would share the belief with his lovely wife that their
money was wisely invested.

Dean Joseph D. Quillian, Jr. has shown us many gracious courtesies. Dr. Albert C. Outler on the occasion of the recognition of Dean Quillian, voiced the esteem many of us felt then—and still feel—for the new leader:

"A scholar respected by scholars, a churchman trusted by churchmen, a man of action whose practical wisdom commends him to men of action. With a nice combination of vision and low-pressure finesse, he has taken up where Dean Cuninggim left off, and has already moved us forward along the same high road."

The courteous consideration shown me by brilliant members of the faculty, and the generous attitude found in the students who spoke out boldly on great issues, brought to me the remembrance of years when I, too, studied there. My appreciation of the ministry was renewed.

Bishop Martin found many other satisfying activities in the 1968-72 period. There were many opportunities for preaching. He delivered three lectureships and conducted preaching missions in several communities. He assisted in presiding at part of an annual conference. Two of the most satisfying events were related to his participation in the services unifying Black and White conferences. One service took place in 1970 when Bishop Kenneth W. Copeland invited him to have a part in the merger in Houston of the Gulf Coast Conference and the Texas Conference. The other was a year later at Centenary College, Shreveport, when Bishop Martin was invited by Bishop Aubrey G. Walton to participate in the merger of Louisiana Conferences A and B. Both occasions were tremendously moving events for him, for he had laid some of the foundations in earlier years for these changes. In another year Bishop O. Eugene Slater invited him to preach at the session of the Southwest Texas Conference.

Bishop and Mrs. Martin observed their Golden Wedding Anniversary in 1970. Members of their family gathered for a dinner in their home. Dr. T. Herbert Minga, pastor of White Rock United Methodist Church, Dallas, had a service for them at the church, with Bishop William C. Martin as the preacher. Mrs. Ray Beene, a friend of many years, entertained with a lovely reception, and Dr. and Mrs. Joseph D. Quillian, Jr., gave another dinner.

Dr. Martin gave the series of Perkins Lectures in 1969, which provided him an opportunity for a real homecoming to First Methodist Church and to Wichita Falls. He brought messages that were warm in spirit and hopeful in tone. Topics for the eight lectures were "Compelling Confidence," "Unsuspecting Enemies," "The Living Past," "The Timeless Injunction," "A Goodly Heritage," "Exacting but Exciting," "The Power of a Great Compulsion," and "Everybody Is Somebody."[3] The lecture on

"The Power of a Great Compulsion" was a careful and unique study of the lives and ministries of several well-known evangelists—Billy Sunday, William Booth, Dwight L. Moody, and Sam Jones. Bishop Martin pointed out limitations and weaknesses in the works of these men but also praised their concern for persons and their dedication to doing God's will as they understood it.[4]

IN RETROSPECT

In looking back over the life and ministry of Bishop Paul E. Martin we must see him within the context of the age in which he lived. In his boyhood church experiences at Blossom he was influenced by an almost universally accepted allegiance to orthodox theological viewpoints. Yet there was little narrowness and no fanaticism involved. In his university years his general intellectual and religious horizons were expanded. In seminary years he was at the beginning of the new stirrings in theology, called liberalism by some and modernism by others. The seminary and the university went through the throes of dismissing two professors, John A. Rice and Mims T. Workman[5] for their "liberalism" in the 1920s. At the time Paul Martin was in the seminary and later serving as a pastor in Dallas. At the beginning of his ministry, the era was hardly gone in which Christians talked about "the evangelization of the world in this generation."

Paul Martin began his adult life as a member of the armed service, during World War I, and he closed his active ministry with the Vietnam conflict still escalating. The great depression of the 1930s was very real to him and to the persons to whom he ministered. Science and technology have changed many patterns of life during his ministry.

In the church itself he has seen the great surge in popularity of religion in the 1950s, followed by a decline in that popularity in the 1960s. He has witnessed the rise of demands for renewal in the church. He has seen numerous short-term splurges of interest in the "suburban captivity of the church," "the death of God," and "the secular city." He has witnessed the impact of numerous religious leaders and thinkers—Rauschenbusch, Niebuhr, Fosdick, and Knox in this country; Barth, Tillich, and Bonhoeffer from abroad; and Rall, Smart, DeWolf, and Outler in the Methodist fold.

He has witnessed the loss of authority on the part of the church in the lives of its own constituency and in society in general. In particular, he has felt the diminishing power and changing role of the bishop in The

United Methodist Church. He has lived into the time of great ecumeni-
city between denominations and between faiths, and the time of religious
and cultural pluralism.

HIS PERSONALITY TRAITS

Against this background, what are the personality traits that Paul E.
Martin brought to bear in seeking to serve his age? He has an even dis-
position, yet not one that would by any means be called dull or stuffy.
On the contrary, he has a flair for the dramatic (but always carefully
controlled to serve his own purposes). This flair came out in the college
pranks of his student days; in adult life he turned this trait into story-
telling (both in and out of the pulpit), and into sermons that were always interesting, and dramatic in Webster's sense: vivid and moving.

There have been some vestiges of his love of fun carried over into
adulthood; one of these is in the telling of funny stories. Another example
is a practice he and his friend, Paul Stephenson, carried on for many
years, even after Paul Martin was a bishop. The two men wore hats that
differed considerably in size; and, particularly when together away from
home, they would trade hats as they walked along the street, Stephenson's
hat coming down to Martin's ears, and Martin's hat just sitting on top of
Stephenson's head. Meanwhile, their wives lagged along behind giggling,
and hoping they would not be identified with the two men ahead of them
toward whom everyone was staring—and smiling.

His nature is one of cheerfulness, optimism, and hopefulness. He has
usually "looked on the bright side of things." J. Frank Dobie said of
another Methodist preacher, the Reverend E. L. Shettles, "He and my
own father have led me to conclude that pure goodness and justice and
mercy and kindness in men make them cheerful."[6] Paul Martin evidently
has in his makeup his share of goodness, justice, mercy, and kindness—
certainly enough to make him cheerful. Some of this hopefulness, of
course, is based on his belief in the power of God to change persons'
lives, not in any belief in man's automatic goodness without God. This
trait has made him friendly, gracious, and courteous. He genuinely likes
people and likes to be liked in return.

Finally, there is in him a drive for perfection. We have seen it in his
careful preparation for every public occasion. "The Bishop loved to
preach and he worked at the job of keeping his preaching fresh, creative,
and helpful," says Dr. Ewing T. Wayland.[7] We have seen it in the careful
way he planned appointments, gathering all the data possible and con-

sidering all the factors involved. We have seen it in the remarkable way he developed friendships, seeking always to make them more than surface pleasantries.

His Life Style

Bishop Martin's way of dealing with persons may be summarized thus: (1) he sought consensus and not controversy; (2) he appealed to the higher motives in persons; and (3) he sought long-range and not short-range solutions and/or results.

His preference for consensus and agreement, rather than for "slugging it out" until one side defeats another, is revealed by his way of operating. One example was the way he helped resolve the issue between the Board of Education and the Board of Publication as to the mode of selecting the editors of church school publications. Rabbi Hyman Judah Schachtel of Houston has said of him, "He doesn't create problems; he solves them." Paul Martin would agree with Ben Franklin, who once wrote to Arthur Lee: "It is true I have omitted answering some of your letters. I do not like to answer angry letters. I hate disputes."[8]

At the same time, the bishop did not shrink from taking a firm position or exercising the power of his office when necessary. Of course, he did not always do this to suit everyone. No bishop, or minister, can please everyone. We have seen indications of this in his "blistering appeal to the members of the Wichita Falls quarterly conference... to wake up from [their]...lethargy," in his "indignation" at the Rio Grande Conference "for sloppiness and work poorly done," in his stand against lawlessness in the Little Rock crisis, and in the witness of several commentators. Ira A. Brumley says: "When a problem came he was willing to use his office to meet it."[9] Another example of the bishop's willingness to act firmly when necessary is reported by Dr. Ewing T. Wayland:

I recall a Methodist minister from the New York Conference who came to Little Rock during the heat of a state-wide "wet-dry" election and who identified himself publicly with the "wets." This came at a time when the Bishop was president of the church's General Board of Temperance. The Bishop was also trying to marshal the church's forces in the state against the "wets," and I might add with considerable success. I managed to get the New York minister in the Bishop's office for a courtesy call. After questioning the visitor about his activities to confirm the public utterances, the Bishop really took him to task and with such effect that the visitor agreed with the Bishop's suggestion that he would get out of the state within the next twenty-four hours. The Little Rock district superintendent and the pastor

of Little Rock's First Church heard this exchange and will vouch for the
Bishop's righteous indignation.[10]

He always tried to appeal to the higher motives in persons, and to
set forth issues in these terms. When asking for large gifts for the church,
Paul Martin always tried to motivate people to give for the sake of the
work of the Kingdom. We have seen an example of his desire to appeal
to higher motives in men and women in the way he dealt with the question of allowing Negroes in the dormitories at Perkins School of Theology. Dr. Wayland writes, "I have never known a person who had the
capacity he had for bringing out the best in those to whom he was related." Dr. Wayland also gives a concrete example:

A group of younger ministers in one of his conferences had been engaged
in some activities and public statements which called into question the direction of the church and some of its concerns. Being the Bishop, he was
properly concerned and took personally the comments of the young ministers. And properly so. Some of the comments were indeed somewhat personal. We had returned late one evening from an engagement. Seated in the
car in the episcopal driveway, he turned to say, "Ewing, what have these
young men got against me? I have tried to do everything I possibly can for
them." And indeed he had, far more than they realized. He was hurt that
these young ministers for whom he was responsible would work at goals different from the goals to which he was totally committed. "Bishop," I replied,
"there is nothing wrong with those young men that a few promotions
wouldn't cure overnight." There was, of course, far more to the situation
than such a simplistic solution. Yet, he continued to work with them, hearing
them out at every opportunity, and, with few exceptions, completely won
them over.[11]

He also sought long-range solutions. In the Little Rock crisis he was
urged to take more immediate and more drastic steps. But he sought
rather to find a reconciling role. Those who know the situation best still
feel that time has proved the wisdom of his course. He managed to hold
together the church, its leadership, and its membership in a time of severe
testing.[12]

Another example of his tactful way of dealing with persons and situations is seen in the manner in which he influenced giving. He grew up
in a time when "raising money" was often done in public meetings, where
recognition, cajolery, and even fear were used to secure large gifts and
small. Bishop Martin, on the other hand, preferred to plant ideas in the
minds of persons, explaining the need to them and showing them a vision

of what a gift would do. He would then let the idea grow until it issued forth as a decision of the giver. It was the difference between stimulating people to give on their own volition and "raising money" from them in spite of their feelings.

His Ministerial Style

As a ministerial and episcopal leader Bishop Martin drove himself hard. He never asked others to give of themselves any more than he demanded of himself. A personal experience of Bishop Robert E. Goodrich illustrates Paul Martin's willingness to work hard and to help others. Some years ago Bob and Thelma Goodrich were to visit the Martins at the home of Mrs. Martin's sister at the Prude Ranch in West Texas. When the Goodriches arrived at the guest cottage where they were to stay they found Paul and Mildred Martin sweeping the cottage floor and making the beds ready for them. No other help was available at the time.[13]

The Martin Teamwork

The Martins worked together, almost as a team, and Mrs. Martin was an important member of the team. One pastor's wife in the Texas Conference wrote the bishop at the time of his retirement, saying, "Mrs. Martin has added sweetness and gentility to your great strengths.... I think you'd have made it on your own, Bishop, but not nearly so well as with Mildred beside you."[14] Another longtime friend wrote the Martins in 1965 and referred to Mildred as "that Fine Little Blossom Queen who bakes your biscuits for you."[15]

At a meeting of the Council of Bishops, in a memoir for one of the wives, reference was made to the number of demands on the wife of a bishop—

the necessity of protecting his health, the necessity of stepping sometimes into obscurity, yet being ever available, the necessity of warding off intrusion, the necessity of utter silence in moments of crisis, the long hours of loneliness, the necessity of quiet encouragement in the face of overwhelming problems, and the necessity of keeping dismay from ever entering the door.[16]

Mildred Martin is universally esteemed as one who meets well all the tests and demands of her exacting role as wife of a minister and bishop. She was the recipient of many honors, including the presidency of the Wives of the Council of Bishops for four years.

Mrs. Martin helped Bishop Martin to keep ever in mind the significant place of the laity in the church. He always sought to enlist them in the great and small tasks that needed to be done. He called upon the laity most frequently in his pastoral years, but he continued to ask for their help during his years as bishop.

OPENING DOORS

He tried as bishop to open doors for ministers and laymen who were ready to step into larger service. For example, he appointed Kenneth Shamblin to Pulaski Heights, Little Rock, and later to St. Luke's Church in Houston; he appointed Robert E. L. Bearden to Fayetteville, from which he was a logical choice by a later bishop to First Church, Little Rock; he appointed Aubrey G. Walton to First Church, Little Rock in 1944, from which he was elected bishop in 1960.

An example of a layman for whom Bishop Martin has opened wider doors is Mr. R. Bryan Brawner, who was an active Methodist in his native Arkansas while Bishop Martin served there. In 1961 he joined the staff of Highland Park Church, Dallas. In 1964, when a new general secretary and treasurer was needed for the Council on World Service and Finance, Bishop Martin (then president of the Council) favored Mr. Brawner, and he became one of the small number of laymen to head a general Methodist agency.

The trait that was most basic to Paul Martin all his life was a pastoral feeling in all situations. It was the result of this trait that led a pastor in Arkansas to write him when he left in 1960: "When I needed you, you were available. I have some letters you wrote me in some trying days, that I shall cherish all my life." It was this trait, undoubtedly, that led Dr. W. F. Bryan in Houston to tell the doctor as he neared death, "Keep me alive till Paul comes." It was this trait that enabled him to form close relationships with men such as Dr. Michael DeBakey, who inscribed a photograph of himself to the Martins that read: "To Bishop Paul E. Martin and Mrs. Mildred Martin, whose inspiring humanitarianism has provided comfort and sustenance to the despairing and has awakened compassion and benevolence in the complacent. With affection and esteem."

RARELY DISAPPOINTED OR EXASPERATED

Being made of flesh and blood, and of emotions, feelings, and reactions, he has, of course. at times been disappointed and exasperated—

though rarely showing it or letting it affect his relationships or decisions. Disappointing experiences would be the result of the occasional failure of some ministers to be fully responsible in their duties, such as keeping appointments and measuring up to their tasks. And he never let his own feelings in such cases influence his treatment of the persons involved.

"He was willing," writes Ira A. Brumley, "to make right any mistake, if he discovered it. He was led once to believe that two men were going around him in a certain very important appointment. He was critical of them, but when he learned the truth he was big enough to let them know that he was in error."[17]

APPOINTMENT-MAKING

We have already noted his care in appointment-making. Throughout his episcopal years he sought to make his appointments the best possible ones. He has commented:

The most exciting responsibility of a bishop is the making of appointments. . . . I found an Old Testament verse, "I sat where they sat" (Ezekiel 3:15), helpful in enabling me to see the situation from the viewpoint of the person being appointed. Many things were dependent on the outcome. Children would be able to go to college because of the proximity. Some members of the family would be able to have needed medical care. A church building program might be set forward. No serious bishop can take lightly such opportunities.

Fortunately, the Bishop has the guidance of the men in his cabinet. They are informed concerning the pastors and their families in their districts. I insisted as we worked together that any prejudice that might exist be eliminated, and I insisted on following a similar discipline myself. A bishop must be careful in forming his judgment. Favoritism must also be avoided.

I have been inspired by unselfish attitudes shown by both ministers and laity in appointment-making. A district superintendent once told me of a minister who offered to move to a smaller appointment in order to make his college-town church available to another minister whose son was ready for college.

At times there are, inevitably, disappointments in assignments. In not a few cases, however, the initial feeling of disappointment changes, at least to acceptance, and sometimes to a more positive attitude.

Appointment-making is one of the bishop's most sacred responsibilities, and deserves his very finest effort.

Bishop Paul E. Martin has summed up much of his conviction about

God, man, and their life together in these words which are an appropriate conclusion for this volume:

Man may walk with a giant step on the moon, but falter and fall on the earth where God has placed him. The mission of the church must be to create a divine fellowship that actually heals the wounds and bridges the chasms that separate one from another.

The church owes the world a steady demonstration of the kind of spiritual unity that is deeper and stronger than loyalty to nation or class or creed. It must lift to the highest possible levels brotherhood, compassion, and love. Prejudice and divisions must be eliminated and unity and brotherhood must be vital parts of this union if it is to be a reality.

Religion must be lifted out of the realm of theory until it becomes a dynamic, verifiable experience [based on] . . . a consuming love for all the children of God.

"Age has brought physical infirmities," reflects Bishop Martin, "but under the care of a skilled physician, who is also a dear friend, Doctor E. Russell Hayes, strength has been renewed and we face the future with confidence. We are forever building!"

Notes

CHAPTER ONE

1. Mrs. W. E. Longstreth, lay delegate from the Missouri Conference, *Daily Christian Advocate*, South Central Jurisdiction, June 16, 1944, p. 10.

2. Clyde Walton Hill, "The Little Towns of Texas," *Shining Trails* (Dallas, 1926).

3. Bishop Martin has written a manuscript entitled "The Humanness of the Ministry: Some Informal Reflections," hereafter referred to as "Reflections." Parts of it are quoted in this book. The entire document is bound and available in Bridwell Library, Southern Methodist University.

4. Letter to the author from Louise Black, September 17, 1972.

5. Martin Papers, Bridwell Library, Perkins School of Theology, Southern Methodist University. Hereafter cited as Martin Papers.

6. A. W. Neville, *The Red River Valley: Then and Now*. (Paris, Texas: North Texas Publishing Company, 1948), p. 77.

7. Letter to the author from Miss Maude Neville, Paris, Texas, January 18, 1973.

8. William A. Owens, *This Stubborn Soil* (New York: Charles Scribner's Sons, 1966), p. 4.

CHAPTER TWO

1. George Sessions Perry, *Texas: A World in Itself* (New York: Whittlesey House, 1942), pp. 4-9.

2. Letter to the author from M. Leo Rippy, August 1, 1972.

3. Letter to the author from Dr. Hemphill Hosford, September 14, 1972.

CHAPTER THREE

1. Letter to the author from Louise Black, September 17, 1972.

2. Letter to the author, July 19, 1972.
3. Letter to the author, July 12, 1972.
4. Minutes, North Texas Conference (1914), p. 55.
5. John M. Moore, *Life and I* (Nashville: Parthenon Press, 1948), pp. 148-49.
6. Martin Papers.
7. Interview with Dr. Walter Towner, August 16, 1972.

CHAPTER FOUR

1. *Journal, North Texas Conference* (1922, 1923, 1924).
2. Interview with Bishop W. Kenneth Pope, November 25, 1972.
3. Ibid.
4. Interview with Bishop Paul E. Martin, June 1, 1972.
5. *History of the North Texas Conference and the Dallas District* (Dallas: Southern Methodist Historical Co., about 1926), pp. 119-20.
6. Interview with Dr. J. Richard Spann, Nashville, Tennessee, August 16, 1972.
7. Interview with Mrs. Miles L. Hines in Iowa Park, November 4, 1972.
8. H. A. Boaz, *Eighty-four Golden Years* (Nashville: Parthenon Press, 1951), p. 194.
9. Letter to the author from Vinson Morris, December 12, 1972.
10. Quarterly Conference Records, Kavanaugh Methodist Church, Greenville, Texas.
11. Ibid.
12. Interview with Marvin Love in Greenville, Texas, November 28, 1972.
13. Letter to the author from Rev. Felix R. Kindel, December 18, 1972.

CHAPTER FIVE

1. Jonnie R. Morgan, *The History of Wichita Falls* (Wichita Falls: Nortex Offset Publications, 1931, 1971), pp. 95-103.
2. Macum Phelan, *A History of the Expansion of Methodism in Texas, 1867-1902* (Dallas: Mathis, Van Nort & Co., 1937), p. 190.
3. Practically all of the data on such details as these in this chapter is taken from the Minutes of the Board of Stewards of the church.
4. Martin Papers.
5. Interview with Mrs. J. J. Perkins, June 2, 1972.
6. Interview with Mrs. J. W. Akin, Jr., November 8, 1972.
7. Interview with Dr. Earl R. Hoggard, November 27, 1972.

CHAPTER SIX

1. Minutes of the Board of Trustees, Southern Methodist University.
2. For further details on this situation see Walter N. Vernon, *Methodism Moves across North Texas* (Dallas: North Texas Conference Historical Society, 1967), chap. 25.
3. The two Martins are not related although Bishop William C. Martin has commented, "Many persons think that Paul and I are brothers. Literally, we are no kin, but in a very real and substantial sense we are. We have enjoyed close relationship during the major part of our lives." (Tape recording to the author, October, 1972).
4. Transcript of taped interview with Bishop A. Frank Smith by Dr. Charles Braden, January, 1962, tape 3, side 2.
5. Ibid.
6. *Book of the Month Club News*, July, 1972.
7. Martin Papers.

CHAPTER SEVEN

1. Data in this chapter is all taken from the Minutes of the Council of Bishops.

CHAPTER EIGHT

1. H. A. Boaz, *Eighty-four Golden Years* (Nashville: Parthenon Press, 1951), p. 182.

2. Ivan Lee Holt, *Eugene Russell Hendrix, Servant of the Kingdom* (Nashville: Parthenon Press, 1950), p. 82.

3. John M. Moore, *Life and I* (Nashville: The Parthenon Press, 1948), p. 158.

4. Letter to the author from Bishop Aubrey G. Walton, October 18, 1972.

5. Letter to the author from Rev. Jolly B. Harper, October 18, 1972.

6. Letter to the author from Rev. E. Clifton Rule, August 24, 1972.

7. Letter to the author from Dr. Ira A. Brumley, August 12, 1972.

8. Martin Papers.

9. *Decisions of the Judicial Council of the Methodist Church* (Nashville: Methodist Publishing House, 1968), 1:150-56.

10. Martin Papers.

11. The quotations from this and other letters to J. Henry Bowdon included in this chapter are used through the courtesy of Dr. Bowdon.

12. Martin Papers.

13. Ibid.

14. Interview with Bishop W. Kenneth Pope, November 25, 1972.

15. Martin Papers.

16. Ibid.

17. Ibid.

18. Interview with Bishop W. Kenneth Pope, November 25, 1972.

19. Ibid.

20. Letter to the author from Dr. Ewing T. Wayland, January 8, 1973.

21. Martin Papers.

22. Ibid.

CHAPTER NINE

1. Walter B. Moore, editor, *Texas Almanac.*

2. George Fuermann, *Reluctant Empire: The Mind of Texas* (New York: Doubleday & Co., 1957), pp. 121-24.

3. Interview with Bishop W. Kenneth Pope, November 25, 1972.

4. Address at the Rio Grande Conference, May 26, 1968, Kerrville, Texas.

5. Letter to the author, December 14, 1972.

6. Ibid.

7. From an address, "What Price, Methodist Reform?" given at the Methodist Conference on Christian Education, Dallas, Texas, November 10, 1967.

8. Martin Papers.

9. Letter to the author, December 14, 1972.

10. *A Journal of Opinion,* published by Ministers for Church Renewal, n.d.

11. *Texas Methodist* (Texas Conference Edition), June 23, 1967.

12. Letter to the author from the Rev. E. Leo Allen, December 19, 1972.

13. Martin Papers.

14. Ibid.

15. Ibid.

16. Ibid.

17. Ibid.

18. Ibid.

19. Ibid.

20. *Daily Christian Advocate,* South Central Jurisdiction, 1960.

CHAPTER TEN

1. *Yearbook, Board of Education, 1952,* p. 732.

2. Ibid, p. 696.

3. Ibid., p. 732.

4. *Quadrennial Reports of the Boards and Commissions of the Methodist Church* (Nashville: Methodist Publishing House, 1952), p. 527.

5. *Proceedings of the Tenth World Methodist Conference, Oslo, Norway, 1961* (Nashville: Abingdon Press).

6. Bishop J. Waskom Pickett, who was the Methodist bishop in Delhi at the time, writes as follows about this visit: "Bishop Martin in his conversation with Prime Minister Nehru made a deep impression, so deep that many times later Mr. Nehru, to whom I introduced between 1944 and 1956 twenty-two Methodist bishops, referred to Bishop Martin more frequently than to any other of our leaders." Letter to the author, April 25, 1972.

7. Letter from Bishop Gerald Kennedy, January 31, 1973.

8. *Daily Christian Advocate*, General Conference of The Methodist Church, 1948, p. 210.

9. Ibid., 1964, p. 384.

10. Ibid., p. 385.

11. Ibid., 1966, p. 981.

12. Ibid., 1968, p. 648.

13. The information in this section is taken from the minutes of the Council as found in its *Yearbook*.

14. *Yearbook, Council on World Service and Finance, 1967-68*, pp. 71-72.

15. *Quadrennial Reports of the Boards and Commissions of The Methodist Church, 1968* (Nashville: Methodist Publishing House, 1968), p. 431.

CHAPTER ELEVEN

1. Letter to the author from Bishop Paul V. Galloway, August 18, 1972.

2. Letter to the author from Dr. Hemphill Hosford, January 7, 1973.

3. "Everybody Is Somebody," Perkins Lectures, 1969.

4. "Saints Wanted," a sermon printed in the *Southwestern Christian Advocate*, February 28, 1935.

5. Letter to the Martins from Mrs. J. J. Perkins, February 5, 1965.

6. John M. Moore, *Life and I* (Nashville: Parthenon Press, 1948), p. 83.

CHAPTER TWELVE

1. Minutes, Board of Trustees, Southern Methodist University, Dallas, Texas. Except as otherwise noted, all such data in this chapter is from the Minutes.

2. Letter from Bishop Paul E. Martin to Bishop William C. Martin, June 8, 1965.

3. Statement by Bishop Paul E. Martin at a luncheon at Perkins School of Theology Alumni at SMU February 3, 1965.

4. Letter from Joe J. Perkins to Bishop and Mrs. Paul E. Martin, July 12, 1944. Martin Papers.

5. Martin Papers.

6. Ibid.

7. Ibid.

8. Transcript of taped interview with Bishop A. Frank Smith by Dr. Charles Braden, January, 1962, tape 3, side 2.

9. Letter to the author from Dr. Hemphill Hosford, December 12, 1972; Dr. Hosford made the presentation on behalf of the university.

CHAPTER THIRTEEN

1. Letter to the author from Dr. Albea Godbold, October 23, 1972.

2. Martin Papers.

3. *Wichita Falls Record News*, March 17, 1969.

4. Tape recording of the lecture, First Methodist Church, Wichita Falls, Texas.

5. For a fuller account of these events see Walter N. Vernon, *Methodism Moves*

across North Texas (Dallas: North Texas Conference Historical Society, 1967), chap. 26.

6. Foreword to *Recollections of a Long Life,* E. L. Shettles (Nashville: Blue and Gray Press, 1973), p. xi.

7. Letter to the author from Dr. Ewing T. Wayland, January 8, 1973.

8. Thomas Fleming, ed., *Benjamin Franklin: A Biography in His Own Words* (New Haven: Philosophical Society and Yale University Press).

9. Letter to the author from Ira A. Brumley, August 12, 1972.

10. Letter to the author from Dr. Ewing T. Wayland, January 8, 1973.

11. Ibid.

12. Concurring in this judgment are Bishop Aubrey G. Walton, Bishop W. Kenneth Pope, and Dr. Ewing T. Wayland.

13. Interview with Bishop Robert E. Goodrich, September 11, 1972.

14. Mrs. James (Ione) Carlin, October 10, 1967, Martin Papers.

15. Letter to the Martins from H. M. Bradford, January 12, 1965.

16. Meeting of the Council of Bishops, November, 1957.

17. Letter to the author from Ira A. Brumley, August 12, 1972.

Index

141